URBAN MIX

EXPLORATIONS OF 8 CROSSINGS AROUND THE WORLD:

MOVEMENTS & INTERACTIONS

Stéphane Lemoine

TABLE OF CONTENTS

TOKYO
ART
109MEN'S
あなたは
恋に溺れる。
TSUTAYA
109MEN'S

WHY MAKE URBAN MOVEMENTS OF CROSSINGS VISIBLE?

After the energy and automobile revolutions, which led to the sprawl of cities and the dislocation of urban spaces,[1] the pandemic has reinforced distancing in cities. However, the increase in the urban and global population, as well as the distances between housing and metropolitan centers, intensify transport and the saturation of the world's metropolises. The fossil fuel crisis is encouraging short trips. A tightening of itineraries is taking place with increasingly complex constraints. From the historical squares of pre-industrial cities for pedestrians and horses, we have moved on to distended intersections with heavy traffic and a multiplication of means of travel, with and without motors. Thus, the need to cross each other increases, but the technical logic of separation and optimization of flows is not sufficient to curb congestion and feelings of insecurity and isolation. This is confirmed by the frequent neglect of multi-modality in the representation of urban intersection management projects, whether it be the latest flow management software such as Aimsun©[2] or research laboratories such as the one at MIT[3]. This is also often the case in the development of autonomous vehicles, which find limits in the first in situ experiments. After the return of the pedestrian and the bicycle in the hierarchy of intersections, it is a question of integrating the diversity of travel modes and augmented mobilities. The idea is to integrate a greater diversity of travel modes by identifying principles that allow for co-presence and not just a hierarchy of presences.

1 "The number of cars, their speed and the gigantism of road infrastructures have made people lose all notion of human scale. The 60 km/h architecture has become dominant, whereas cities were previously shaped by a 5 km/h architecture." Jan Gehl, interview with midionze.com on April 23, 2013.

2 Aimsun is a French traffic simulation software.

3 An animation from the research program led by Carlo Ratti Drivewave/Senseable City Lab/MIT, in 2016, presents the end of traffic lights by proposing an intersection with a continuous movement of cars in an urban neighborhood in Boston, forgetting about pedestrian crossings.

For several decades, sociologists have been emphasizing the need for people to meet. Mobility specialists have clearly identified the importance of train stations as places where people cross one another and change ways of moving. The handling of crossroads calls attention to the human scale allowing for co-presence and encounters, and not just the fluidity of masses. The conception of the movements makes it possible to integrate the possibility of crossing others, or not, according to local practices and activity. This is therefore a new indicator of quality. The greater the diversity of crossroads, the more exchange is favored.

Social approaches also insist on modes of travel that correspond to lifestyles. Thus, the design of intersections must leave room for freedom of movement and, by extension, the choice of lifestyles. The ability to choose allows the possibility

4 Gayet-Viaud, Carole, 2022, *La civilité urbaine, Les formes élémentaires de la coexistence démocratique*, Economica, collection études sociologique.

for meeting and exchange. The public spaces that allow this are urban, in the sense that they allow civility.[4] The urban square has specific codes that allow people to move around while paying attention to others and understanding their situation in a high-density residential area. The crossroads is the place of a diversity of cultures that qualify the movements. The more the diversity of the intersections is explored, the more the logic and complexities of urban movements will be known in favor of the freedom of "crossed" movement, a freedom relative to the diversity of movements and to the respect between the mobile elements that cross. Our interest lies in the connection to others and our surroundings in the term “culture”.

The complexity of intersections is an urban quality to be understood in order to better live in the city and make it evolve according to frequentation.

APPROACH

This survey presents the movements of users in the city at the scale of an intersection and a few minutes.

The representation of all movements simultaneously, the spatial and temporal constraints and the attitude of the users are explored as a whole. The aim is to represent the dynamic and perceived phenomena in an urban space from filmed, photographed and drawn data. It is a visit to squares and what animates them, an investigation of the quality of movements and not of spaces.

A lot of data is available on flows, but most often with a quantitative purpose used to optimize the speed of movement. GPS navigators are primarily designed to connect point A to point B in the shortest possible time, and they do not provide information on the dynamics and diversity of movements in the city. To explore these phenomena, we focused on the most complex situation in urban movements: intersections. We analyzed several squares around the world from data available on the web in March 2020, collected during the period of confinement due to Covid.

The approach is situated between the disciplines of dynamic cartography, urban anthropology, analysis of flows, travel patterns, land organization and landscape. It does not deal with social categories, transport infrastructures, individual expectations, traffic capacities or territorial planning and governance. This approach, between mobility and urban planning, aims to produce new information on the diversity and density of urban spaces. The consideration of what moves in a city is called the "urbanism of movements".

The hypotheses of this exploration are as follows:

– At the center of the saturation of the world's major metropolises, inhabitants cross paths with flexible logics linked to their mode of travel and culture. They reveal inclusive tactics of movement, essential to urban activity and attractiveness.

– The lack of representation of the diversity and detail of movements in city centers makes it impossible to understand the conditions of urban quality based on crossing, at the human scale. It seems necessary to produce new representations of flows in the city, closer to lived perceptions

– New illustrations of intersections provide insight into different types of crossing. These discoveries are useful for the design of increasingly busy urban spaces in order to mix the greatest possible diversity and freedom of movement, vital to urban exchanges, as understood by the economist Melvin Weber in 1963 in his definition of urban (intensity of exchange)[5] and the sociologist Roger Clausse, the same year, with the idea of the social need for relationships (the connection).[7].

– The connection to others and to the context allows us to understand the logic of users who cross differently depending on the country.[7].

5 Webber, Melvin, 1996, *L'urbain sans lieu ni bornes*, La Tour d'Aigues, éd de L'aube (translation from "The Urban Place and the Nonplace Urban Realm", 1963).

6 Bolle De Bal, Marcel, *Reliance, défiance et liance, émergence de trois notions sociologiques*, 2003, in Sociétés 2003/2 no. 80, 99-131, De Boeck Supérieur, Cairn.info.

7 Descola, Philipe, 2021, *Les Formes du visible: Une anthropologie de la figuration*, Paris, Seuil.

At the beginning

The effects of mobility on the city have structured it, from crossing roads at its origin to highway interchanges, leading to its dissolution. Within the AP5 agency and for more than 15 years, we have been exploring the impacts of mobility on urban configurations and public spaces in the context of operational urban projects. Central squares and events are emblematic of cities, marked by the quantity and quality of traffic. Knowing that the perception of movements strongly impacts the understanding of the city and its transformation, how can we qualify the frequentation of emblematic sites of the city?

At the same time, visits to major world cities have raised questions about the organization of crossroads and of different atmospheres. How can we account for the variations in behavior observed on each site?

The tools of urban planning are often restricted with fixed views from above, without any relation to the users' feelings and in a hierarchical and safe approach to modes of transport. The composition of the space is conditioned by the internal logic of the projects implemented and limited to their perimeter. They often seem to be disconnected from the characteristics of the flows of the various mobile elements in the city.[8] The planning of spaces and circulation does not always take into account existing and future polarities and the links to be established between them. Information on flows on a human scale, routes between centers, variations in use, gauges, the multiplicity of modes, temporalities, speeds and the possibility of stopping is often missing from the foundations of urban projects. The consideration of mobile movements is often restricted to a criterion of fluidity. Data is beginning to develop, but there is little synthetic information. The understanding of a set of movements in the city and their effects requires new representations, synthesis documents in addition to dynamic tools.[9]

8 By mobile elements we mean anything that moves in the intersection, i.e., a pedestrian or a vehicle, sometimes carrying a variable number of passengers or goods.

9 Lemoine Stéphane, *Partager la conception, inviter à imaginer*, p. 78, 2010, Dessine-moi une ville, collective work under the direction of A. Masboungi, Editions du Moniteur and courses on dynamic representations of the city at the École Nationale Supérieure d'Architecture de Paris Malaquais in 2013.

Finally, the AP5 agency took part in a full-scale experiment to make 10 events accessible for 24 hours in Ile de France. This project questioned the mobility of travellers through different trajectories, from modes of transport to mobility assistants. Tactics and abilities of visitors appeared, creating atmospheres of movement, beyond the contexts.[10]

10 La grande ville 24 heures chrono, 2012, Ministère de la culture et de la communication/ Bureau de la recherche architecturale, urbaine et paysagère, Cité de l'architecture, Recherche-action experimental programme.

These observations and experiences are at the origin of this book.

The choice of intersections

For this exploration, we have selected sites around the world to visit the diversity of configurations and possibilities, and to confront the ambiences.

Taking at least one example per major cultural and continental bloc, the first selection criterion is geographical: Asia, Africa, the Americas, Europe, India, China. Oceania and North America have been omitted for the time being, with only 8 sample sites.

In order to refine the choice with comparable urban case studies, we have retained the following common points on each site:

- the over-frequentation of the site, a phenomenon of crowding and mixing (several thousand people per day),
- the mixing of travel modes,
- dimensions of non-built space of approximately 50 m x 50 m (3-minute pedestrian crossing time),
- the intersections are flat, without any separation of the flows by level, in order to increase interactions and crossroads,
- a central location in the selected metropolises and an internationally recognized place,
- the availability of sufficient information on the internet in March 2020.[11]

11 The web sources used are listed at the end of the book.

We have also taken care to retain different configurations, but above all with a strong singularity in the organization of the intersection and the local relationship to mobility. The traffic light and roundabout models are the basic plans, but with a specific deformation for each site. We noted the following specificities:

- Old Delhi/Hauz Qasi Chowk in India; a bustling old intersection, multi-modal and with small vehicles and animals,
- Copenhagen/Rådhuspladsen at Denmark; the capital of cycling,

- Tokyo/Shibuya crossing in Japan; one of the busiest pedestrian intersections in the world,
- Hanoi/Dong Kinh Nghia Thuc Square in Vietnam; high traffic flow without regulation,
- London/Oxford Circus in England; an inclusive multi-modal intersection in Europe,
- Lagos/Ojuelegba and Alagbede-Igbobi Road and A1 intersection in Nigeria; the saturation of the intersection which multiplies exchanges,
- Sao Paulo/Av. Brigadeiro g Faria Lima and Av. President Juscelino Kubitschek in Brazil; a left-turn free intersection with a checkerboard layout, a road model with the insertion of a new axial bicycle lane,
- Beijing/Chengfu and Zhongguancun E crossroads in China; an XXL intersection with alleyways and a checkerboard layout.

The outline

The first part of this book proposes a link between mobility and movement to address urban quality in our overcrowded cities.

The second part presents the 8 sites in order to explore the movements of all the mobile elements over the time of day and a 3-minute sequence. The spatial configuration and the polarities have been drawn for each site. The aim is to further understand the variations and tactics of movements.

The third part proposes synthetic representations of movements in order to capture the qualitative dimensions specific to each site studied. These images contribute to the understanding of the organizations experienced, in contrast to the usual representations that are numerical, abstract and off-site.

The last part opens up new avenues for the transformation of intersections into inclusive and comfortable urban spaces for all mobile users, residents and visitors.

I
FROM MOBILITY TO THE URBAN

From mobility to movement variations

Travel is constantly increasing in urban areas. In order to better respond to the expectations and comfort of inhabitants, the approach of specialists has changed from a vision of "transport", linked to the ability to move a majority of people in the simplest way, to that of "mobility", linked to people with their own motivations and multiple journeys. Thus, people's movements are dependent on their motivations, the places they go, the information available and the means that enable them to travel. The organization of travel in the territory has opened up to the diversity of people and the "mix" of travel modes.[12] .

12 "Do the right mix ", European Union awareness program, September 2012.

Leaving aside transport infrastructures or a quantitative and speed-related approach, this work presents the elements in motion on a site. We propose here to zoom in on intersections to focus on the places where people pass, meet, exchange and rub shoulders in the city. The variation of flows and the management of intersections vary greatly from country to country. Fluctuations in speed, traffic lights, roundabouts, separate crossings, but also the management of priorities by the kind of mobility, influence movements. The devices used for crossings modify the flows but also the attitude of the user, as well as the perception of his/her neighbourhood. Beyond the respect of rules and the ingenuity of the management of crossings, the trajectories and rhythms of people have been observed to understand habits, reflexes or even accidents throughout the world.

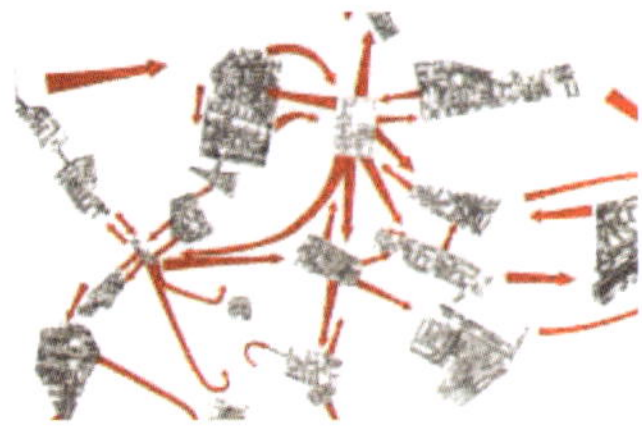

Debord, Guy, May 1957, Psychogeographical Guide to Paris, *Discourse on the Passions of Love, Psychogeographical Slopes of the Drift and Location of Ambient Units*, pamphlet published by the Situationist Bauhaus, printed by Permild & Rosengreen, Copenhagen.

Excerpt from a photograph by André Kertész, Washington Square with snow, February 24, 1966.

The crossing of thousands of people every day is site-specific. Respecting the rules varies depending on the culture and the reasons for mobility. How does this happen? What are the organizations and variations that allow for the mixing of movements and therefore of mobile elements?

A lack of attendance representation in the public space

The quality of a square comes from its history, its inhabitants, its organization, its fullness and emptiness, its climate, but also from its activity. The passage of users through a square offers a spectacle of the city's inhabitants, but also gives the opportunity to move, to meet and to show themselves. The inclusion of all these presences is achieved through the various and varied movements in the same space at different times and the possibility of crossing. What data exists on the beauty and diversity of movement in an urban square and on the mix of modes of travel (by car, on foot, by bike, in a truck, in a stroller, ...)? While some architects such as Louis Kahn[13] or Junya Ishigami have already designed architectures based on the survey of movements, few representations show the observation of the qualities of existing movements on a square, apart from texts and photographs. The analysis of typical behaviors by sociologists or engineers often aims to isolate and then standardize movements. Perspective represents a point of view, the 2D image is static, the temporal patterns of geographers are complex and the frequency tables of engineers are uniform. For cartography, the scale close to experience is not obvious and the detail of movements is difficult to represent.[14] We are therefore looking for traces of the combination of movements, of the co-presence and diversity of movements in a public space.

13 Louis I. Kahn's Traffic Study project, Philadelphia 1952, Junya Ishigami's project for the Kanagawa Institute of Technology 2011, or Bernard Tschumi's 1981 concept of kinetics.

14 The need to represent trajectories is noted by Offner, Jean-Marc, 2020, *Anachronisme urbains*, Presses de SciencesPo.

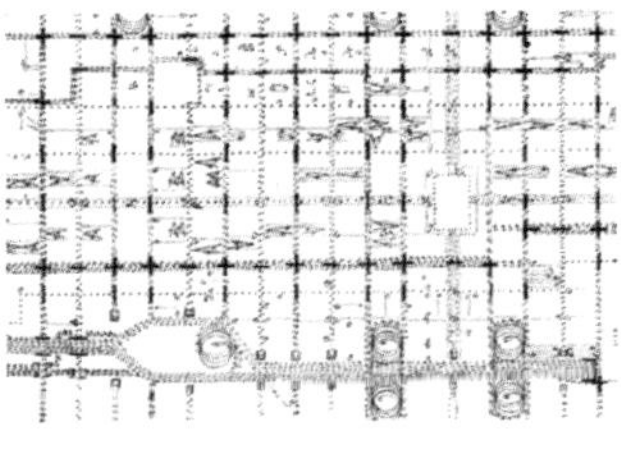

Excerpt from the plan of the Louis I. Kahn Traffic Study project, Philadelphia 1952.

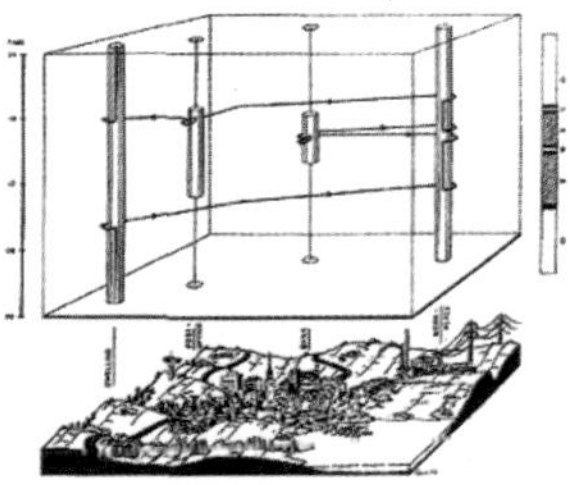

Figure of the temporal path on a territory, from Hagerstrand's time geography, diagram extracted from Lentrop, A Time-Geographic Simulation Model of Individual Activity Programs, in *Timing Space and Spacing Time* by Carlstein, D. Parkes and N. Thrift (Eds.), Human activity and time geography, London, Edward Arnold, 1978, pp. 162-180.

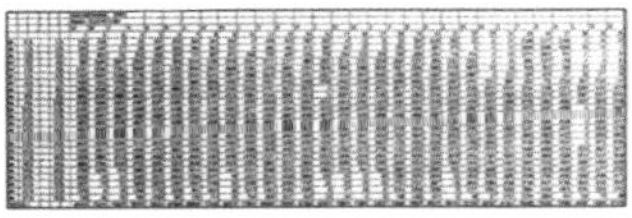

Table of figures, Survey of the station S A3W2.200 (magnetic sensor) traffic per hour, month of November 1994, Traffic table on the A3 motorway in Bondy, Ile-de-France, DREIF.

Beyond traffic signals, what do we know about the particularities of intersections between different metropolises in the world? What representations speak of the specificities of movements between Hanoi and Copenhagen? Are movements more numerous, more pleasant, more varied, richer in some places than in others?

Efficient intersections at public squares

The paradigms that guide the approach to mobility are often reduced to speed, time and cost. This quantification of mobility thus sets aside the other factors that motivate and qualify it: the diversity of motives for travel, the possibility of meeting other people, the integration of new practices within mobility spaces and the diversity of travel modes.[15] These qualities, which are generally recognized as those of public spaces, are often excluded or forgotten in spaces reserved for travel. For intersections, which are of interest to us here, we propose to look at them by paying attention to all the variations in the trajectories of mobile elements and crossings. Avoiding specializing on one mode and defining the best conditions for each mode separately, we observe the interactions between all mobile elements. The inclusion of all the modes, of encounters, deviations, inflections, variations in speed, temporal fluctuations in frequentation, changes in functioning, mixing and sharing, corresponds to the definition of a living and animated square.[16] Thus, we are looking for the ability to integrate diversity, micro-accidents between mobile elements, temporal adaptations and new practices in the intersections. It is a question of complementing the multiple and mythical narratives of urban walks[17] to speak of the animation and diversity of a square, as a whole. Putting aside the security and quantitative approach, we focus on the deformations of the system and its capacity to integrate the unexpected. The identification of movements in the city aims to capture the urban quality factors of public squares.

15 Paul Amar, in his role as a prospectivist*, proposes new trends for mobility based on the qualities of use and experience, and not just efficiency. - Amar, Georges, 2010, *Homo Mobilis, Une civilisation du mouvement*, Fyp édition.

16 An example with the impressionist painting of Parisian crossroads: The French Theatre Square, 1898, Oil on Canvas, Camille Pissarro.

17 Two examples among many: Gracq, Julien, *La forme d'une ville*, 1985, Corti, or Benjamin, W., les passages de Paris, 1934, Cerf.

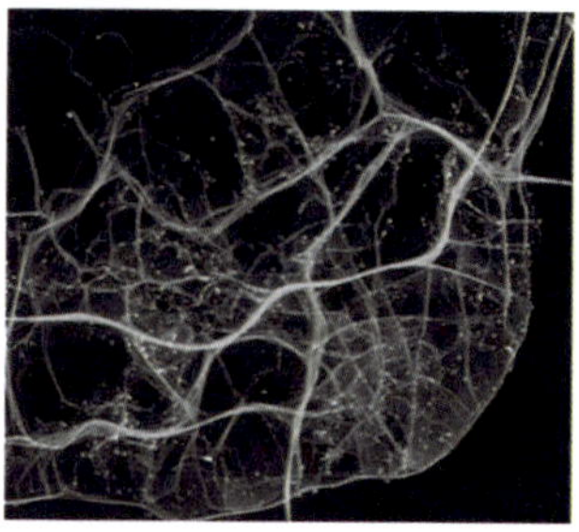

Cruz, Pedro Miguel, 2010, Maps and animations of taxi traffic in Lisbon by fluidity, www.mitportugal.org.

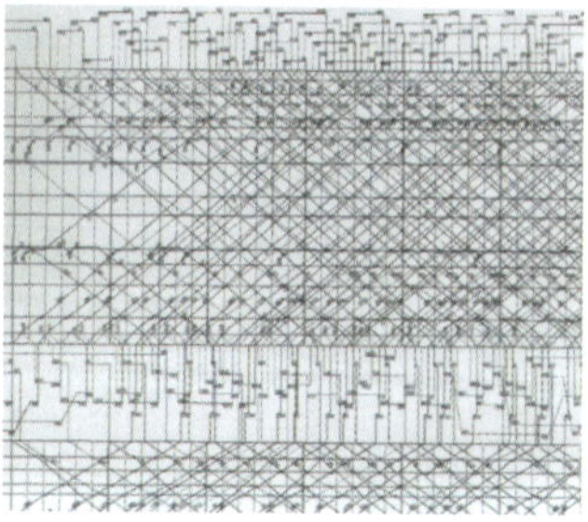

Timetable, Operation diagram for 12:00 noon, July 25, 1985, Tokaido and Sanyo Shinkansen Lines (bullet train), Japanese National Railroad control room, Tokyo. In Tufte 1990©.

Duomo pedestrian square in Milan, 2022 © Googlemaps.

A condition for urban quality: crossings

If the appreciation of a site can be subjective, passing in a place can cause pleasant meetings or accidents. This experience, according to the trajectories, motives, modes of travel or even appointments, strongly marks the perception of a place. We are not talking here about the emotional and social state, which has been extensively dealt with by anthropologists and sociologists,[18] but about the ability to move in a square according to the observed movements.

18 Hall, E.T., 1966, *The Hidden Dimension*, New York, Knopf Doubleday. And more recently with Stéphane Juguet and Stéphane Chevrier, who are not unseasoned travelers, RATP 2012.

The diversity of movements sought on the sites appears with the possibility of crossings and co-presence of modes of transport. If automation, standardization or limitation of movements can be a factor of exclusion, the richness of encounters is favored by the possibility of crossing. The exploration of movements in a crossing shows how this urban activity is made possible every day in large metropolises.

This urbanity in the comfort of movement has been developed a lot in the last few decades, notably with Jan Gehl[19] for the pedestrian, after the first explorations by Kevin Lynch[20] for the car. On a human scale, these daily demonstrations of the intensity of exchanges are concrete proof of responsiveness. The mixing of modes requires a capacity to manage the crossing by each user and common codes. The initiative* of making large historic squares pedestrian is also to be sought in multi-modal squares, from the village to the metropolis, which are also places of destination to be made pleasant.

19 Gehl, Jan, 2013, *For Cities on a Human Scale*, Montreal, éditions Ecosociété.

20 Lynch, Kevin, Appleyard, Donald, 1964, *The View from the Road*, MIT press.

We are therefore going to look for indications to transform a traffic intersection into an urban square.

Time-lapse photograph by Martin Roemers, New M.A. Jinnah Road, Saddar Town, Karachi, Pakistan 2015.

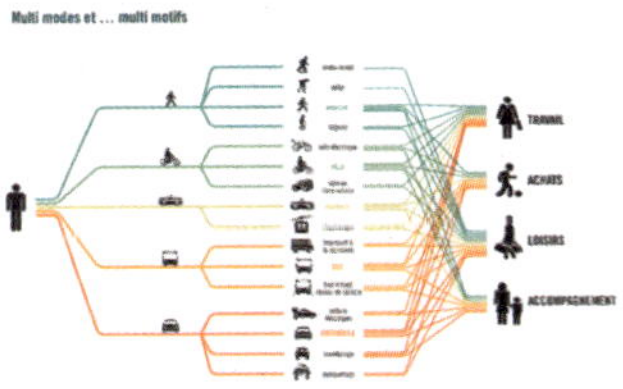

Diagram on modes, motives and trajectory crossings, Mobility consultation on the territory of Clermont-Ferrand, 2015 © APS.

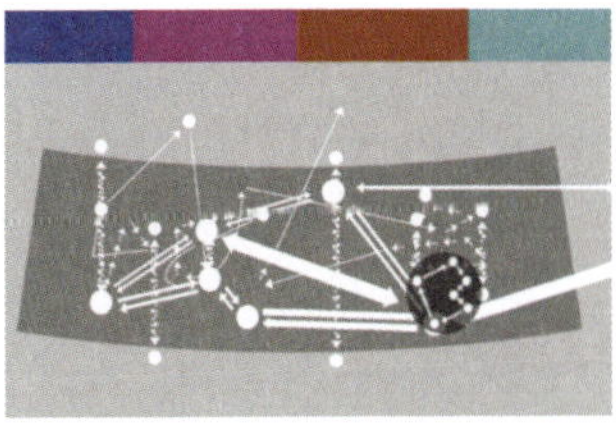

Typologies of movement of the inhabitants on the coast of Saint Nazaire, France, 2012 © APS.

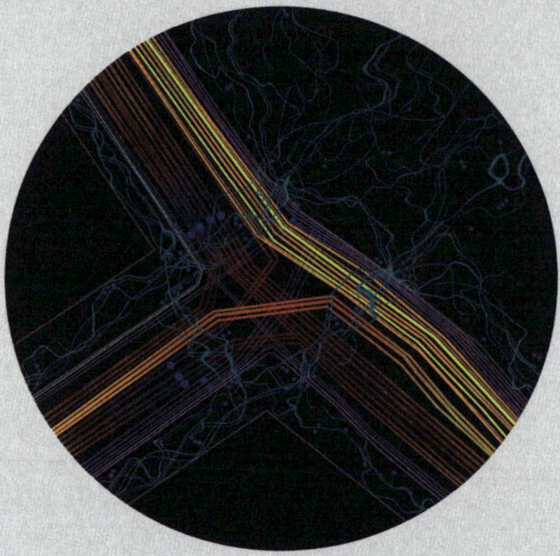

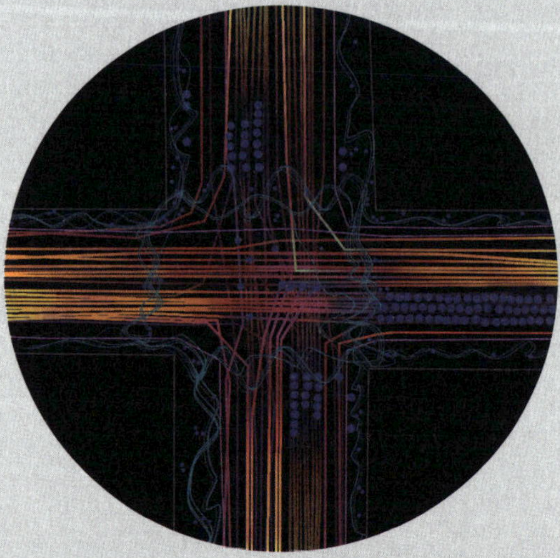

II
VARIATIONS ON 8 INTERSECTIONS

This second part presents the spatial configurations and the movements of the mobile elements* over a 3-minute sequence for the following 8 intersections:

- Old Delhi / India
  Hauz Qasi Chowk
- Copenhagen / Denmark
  Rådhuspladsenau
- Tokyo / Japan
  Shibuya crossing
- Hanoi / Vietnam
  Dong Kinh Nghia Thuc Square
- London / England
  Oxford Circus
- Lagos / Nigeria
  Ojuelegba and Alagbede-Igbobi Road and A1 intersection
- Sao Paulo / Brazil
  Av. Brigadeiro g Faria Lima and Av. President Juscelino Kubitschek
- Beijing / China
  Chengfu and Zhongguancun E crossroads

For each of the sites, the following was drawn and specified:

- The aerial view of the intersection.
- The spatial configuration showing the distribution of public open spaces in relation to the built-up area, the sharing of public space (roadway, sidewalks, plantings, lanes reserved for a specific mode) and the main polarities (shops, train station, metro station, or public facilities).
- A cross-section in the middle of the crossroads shows the distribution of mobile elements therein (grouped by mode or mixed).
- The modal share and number of mobile* elements relate to the roundabout only during a 3-minute sequence.
- A record of the traffic with details of the different modes per intersection at two points in time (low traffic, high traffic).
- Diagrams showing the different movement tactics observed.

*A mobile element should be understood as a unit in motion, regardless of the number of people carried in vehicles.

Legend of the mobile elements

Graphical study of simultaneous speed differences © AP5, 2020

01 OLD DELHI / HAUZ QASI CHOWK IN INDIA
The site is in the old center and leads to the city's most flourishing markets. An underground subway serves the square with two exits on the sidewalks. Rickshaw drivers often flood the square while waiting for customers. Amidst the vehicle traffic, street vendors set up stalls to capture passersby. Sometimes cows and buffaloes cross the street.

02 COPENHAGEN / RÅDHUSPLADSEN IN DENMARK
The intersection is located in the downtown area near the main town hall square and various equipment, office, and commercial buildings. The square is a popular destination for gatherings. Located on H. C. Andersens Boulevard, there is significant automobile, pedestrian and bicycle traffic.

03 TOKYO / SHIBUYA CROSSING IN JAPAN
Shibuya is one of the busiest intersections in the world with up to 2,500 pedestrians moving at the same time and every day. The area is home to many restaurants, shopping malls, offices and entertainment venues. The intersection is located next to Shibuya Station, one of the busiest metropolitan rail hubs in the capital. The large number of public transportation users crowds the intersection day and night.

04 HANOI / DONG KINH NGHIA THUC SQUARE IN VIETNAM
Located in the historic city center, the square supports a continuous flow of mopeds. The 5-branch intersection is located next to Hoan Kiem Lake, several shopping areas, markets and hotels.

05 LONDON / OXFORD CIRCUS IN ENGLAND
At the junction of Regent and Oxford Streets, this intersection is a popular shopping destination with heavy car and pedestrian traffic throughout the day. Added to this, is the pedestrian traffic from the underground station, located just below the intersection. A crosswalk in the center allows for diagonal crossing. The narrow traffic lanes limit the speed of vehicles and their number. The intersection has been transformed to accommodate the heavy pedestrian, car, taxi and bus traffic.

06 LAGOS / OJUELEGBA AND ALAGBEDE-IGBOBI ROAD JUNCTION AND A1 IN NIGERIA
The site is an important public transport hub with buses and shared motorbikes. It is a commercial district, with sedentary and itinerant merchants. It is crossed by a highway viaduct, linking Lagos Island to the mainland. It is reputed to be the most congested intersection in the country.

07 SAO PAULO / AV. BRIGADEIRO G FARIA LIMA AND AV. PRESIDENT JUSCELINO KUBITSCHEK IN BRAZIL
The intersection is close to the financial district of the Brazilian capital. The streets connect the headquarters of various multinational companies. To meet the needs of employees and executives, many restaurants, banks, bars, business hotels are present. The particularity is to have an axial bicycle path, in the middle of a vast road crossing.

08 BEIJING / CHENGFU AND ZHONGGUANCUN E CROSSROADS IN CHINA
Next to Tsinghua University, the intersection is surrounded by large educational centers, with many residential and commercial programs.
The intersection has a classic geometry with wide dimensions and high multi-modal traffic. The modes are clearly separated on the streets.

Noises and movements all over the place

Attractors and attractions
Numerous itinerant merchants and shop extensions invade the streets and pavements. This often causes crowds in the middle of the square. Several public buildings and shops are important fixed attractors, in addition to the large nearby markets.

Modes
Cars, motorcycles, tempos (mini-trucks), bicycles, rickshaws and electric rickshaws, pedestrians and animals share the public space. It is a homogeneous distribution of modes with a lot of diversity and a majority of pedestrians.

Activities
The barges and animals cause slowdowns for vehicles.

Modal share

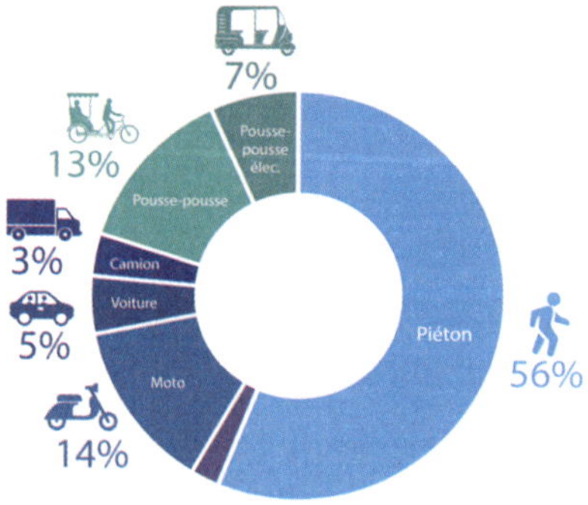

Elements in movement

270/3mn

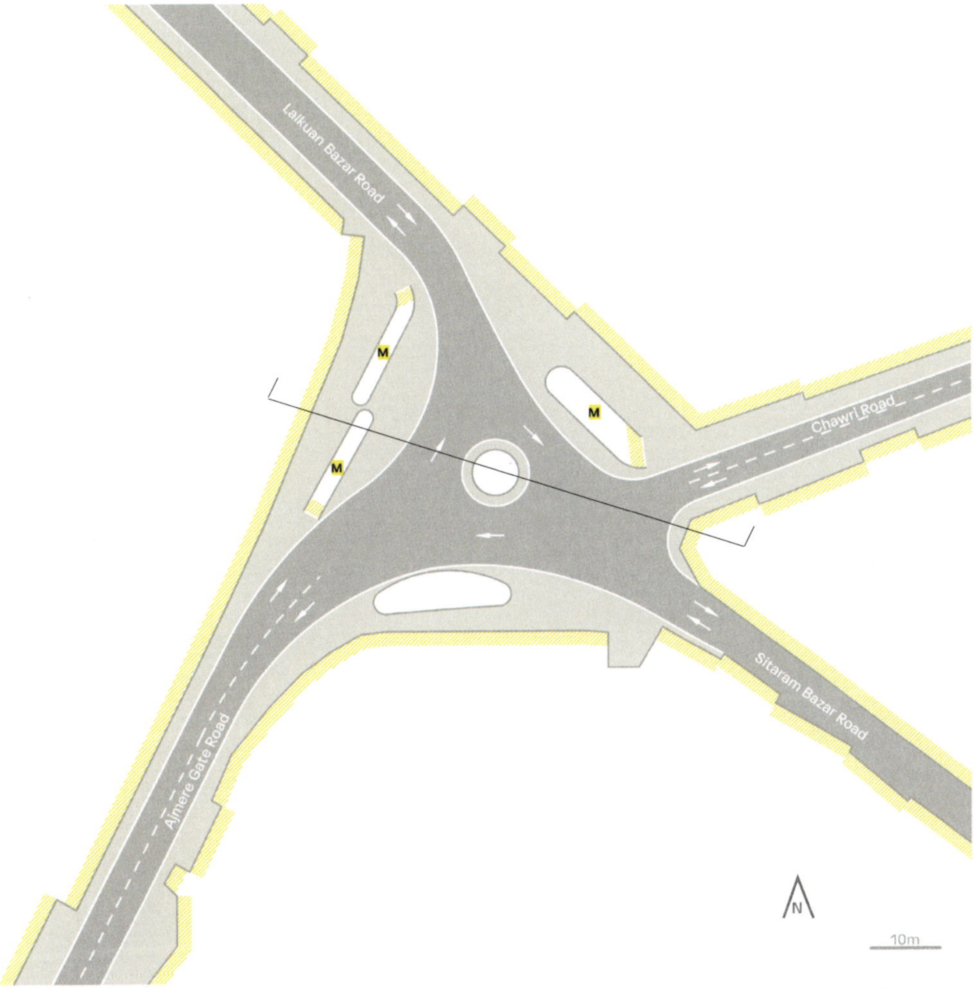

support

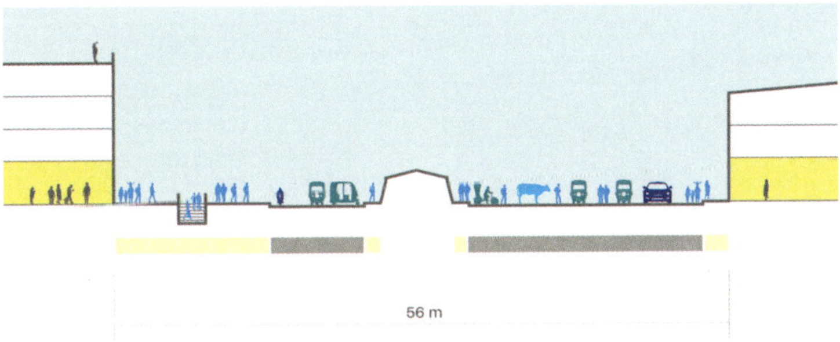

elevation

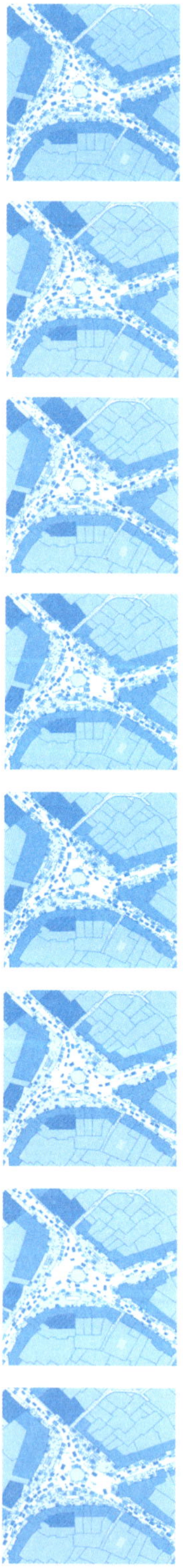

Attendance over a period of 3 minutes

Small roundabout

MINIMUM ACTIVITY
05H00

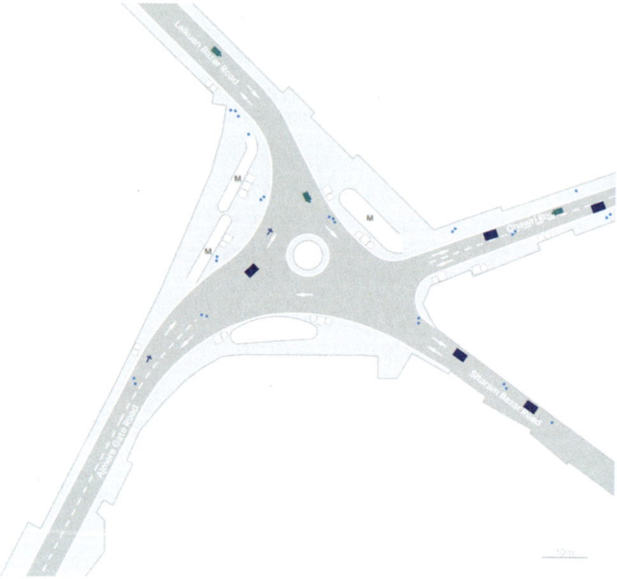

Bus
Truck
Car
Bike
Electric rickshaw
Rickshaw
Bicycle
Rollerblading, skateboarding and scootering
Pedestrian
Animal
Mobile stationa

MAXIMUM ACTIVITY
14H00

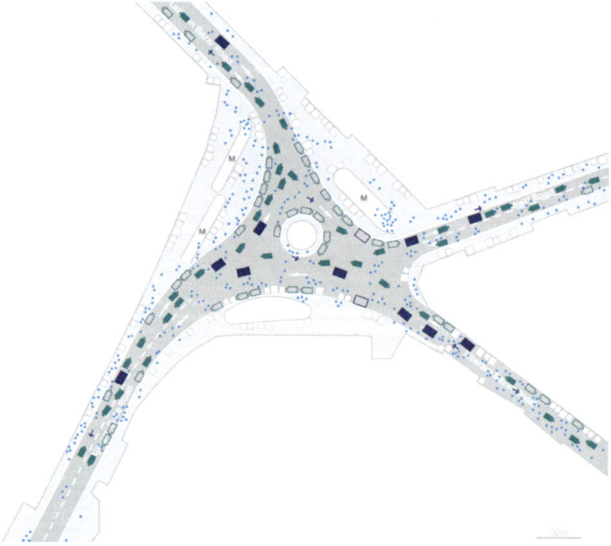

and self-regulation

Variations of movements

All streets operate in both directions, regardless of width. On narrow streets, when crossing, eye contact between drivers signals the direction they will take in relation to each other. Vehicles drive on the left.

With the absence of dedicated crossings, pedestrians often cross streets anywhere, abruptly and regardless of the proximity of the approaching vehicle. Honking is therefore a common phenomenon to indicate to the pedestrian the danger of crossing paths and the request to leave the street clear.

Pedestrians can cross from one stall to another in an impromptu manner and zigzag through the intersection.

The mix of vehicles of different sizes and their numbers often causes unpredictable movements. As a result, drivers must adopt a slow speed and brake often.

The particularity of this intersection with a small roundabout is that there is no imposed timing, nor reserved passageways. As such, during the 3-minute sequence, all the movements are possible by taking care to weave through the mobile elements and possibly to stop for a purchase.

Tactics of movements diagrams

The continuous traffic flow of vehicles and pedestrians sometimes causes chaos due to poor coordination, resulting in traffic jams and thus many breaks in movement. However, the small size of the vehicles often makes it possible to escape after a few attempts.

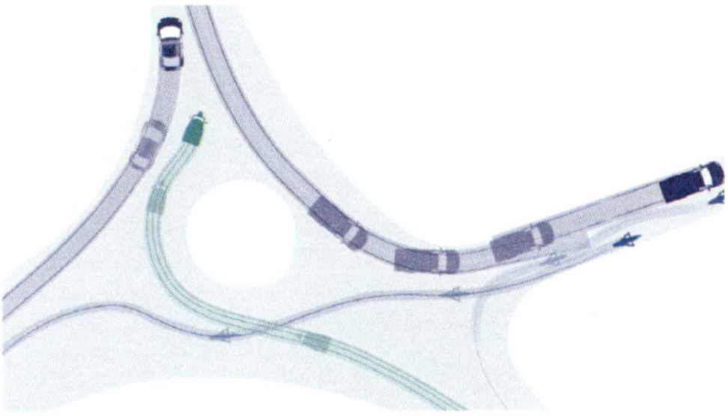

1. Vehicle movements are slow and jerky to avoid collision with other moving vehicles.

2. Itinerant shops act as an attraction and cause crowds around their improvised location, even to the point of disrupting the adjacent traffic.

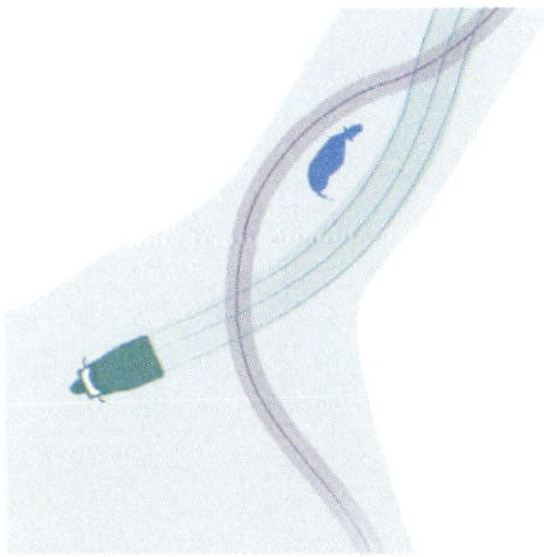

3. Movement is unpredictably disrupted by sacred animals running loose in the middle of the tracks, which do not respect the right-hand right of way.

Precise organization to relax in

<u>Attractors and attractions</u>
The town hall and the historic square are close to many shopping centers, restaurants and hotels. This makes the square an important meeting place. The shops and restaurants in the streets attract locals, employees, and tourists.

<u>Modes</u>
Bicycles are the preferred mode of travel. Separate lanes for bicycles allow for fast and continuous movement alongside pedestrians and vehicles. The modal split represents a balance between motorized vehicles and soft modes.

<u>Activities</u>
A lot of traffic is observed in the morning, as many people go to work and to cafes to have breakfast. Many shops also open at this time. This traffic continues throughout the day.

Modal share

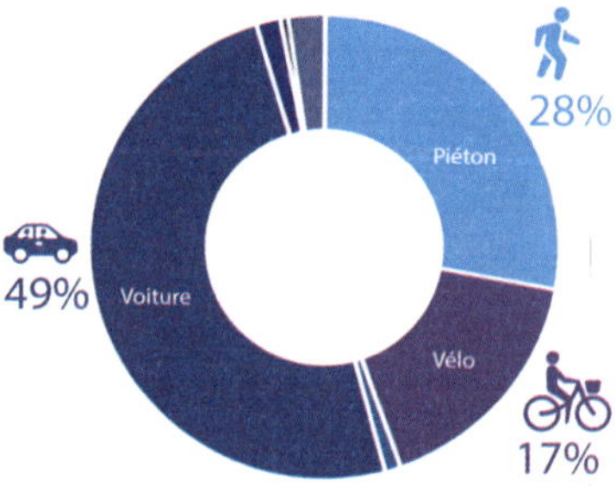

Elements in movement

270/3mn

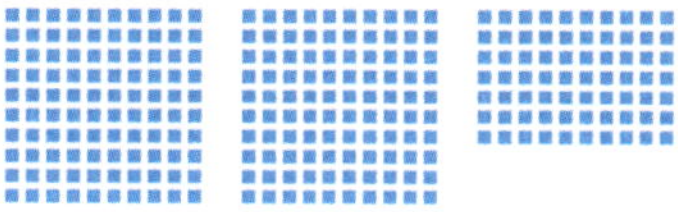

support

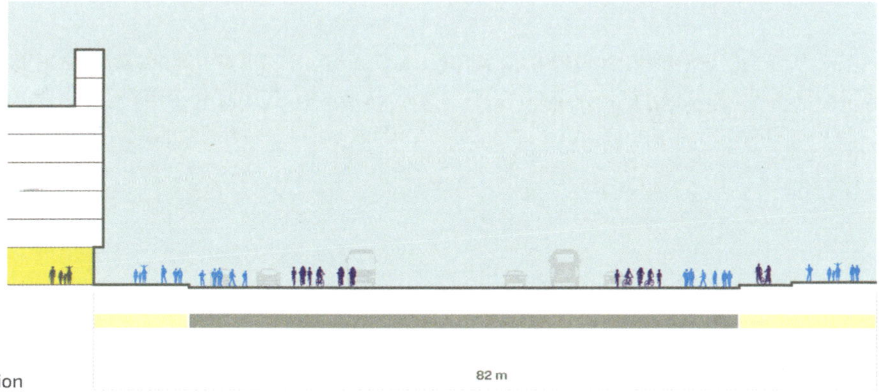

elevation

4-phase Regulation

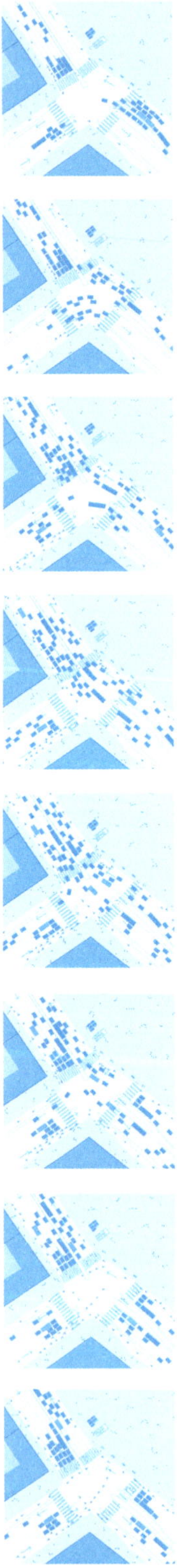

Attendance over a period of 3 minutes

MINIMUM ACTIVITY
05H00

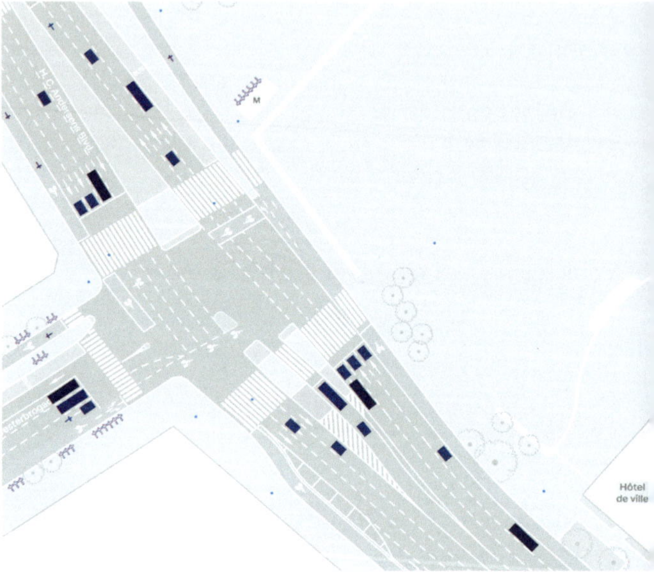

Bus
Truck
Car
Bike
Electric rickshaw
Rickshaw
Bicycle
Rollerblading, skateboarding and scootering
Pedestrian
Animal
Mobile station

MAXIMUM ACTIVITY
10H00

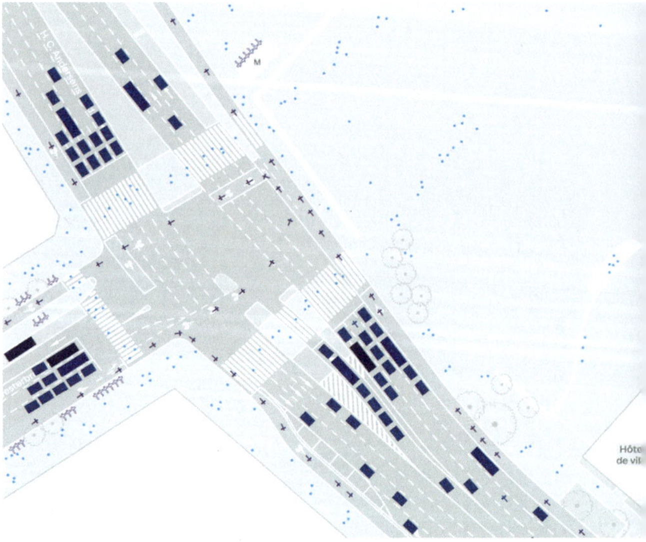

Variations of movements

The lowest attendance is observed in the early morning.

Most pedestrian areas are wide and have uninterrupted traffic flow. Pedestrians and vehicles strictly respect sidewalks and crossings. Various dividers are present along the street. Pedestrians prefer to wait for the next green signal and obey the rule, rather than take advantage of the traffic interruption.

Vehicles have their headlights on during all hours of the day.

This traffic light intersection is very organized with a time for pedestrians, bicycles and vehicles. Bicycle movements are facilitated because the intersection is equipped with a light that provides a specific time for their passage. Cyclists must stop to turn left and give way to pedestrians.

The intelligent traffic light system modifies the duration of a particular movement according to traffic variations.

Tactics of movements diagrams

The movement management is precise and very complete, with multiple movements taking place together, but limiting the crossings.

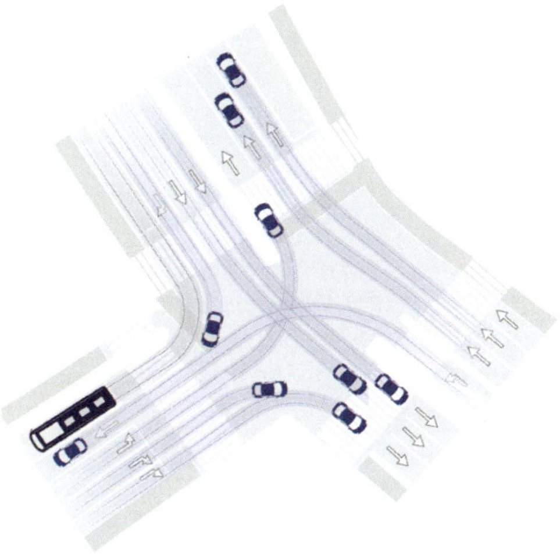

1. Motor vehicles have separate lanes for changing direction.

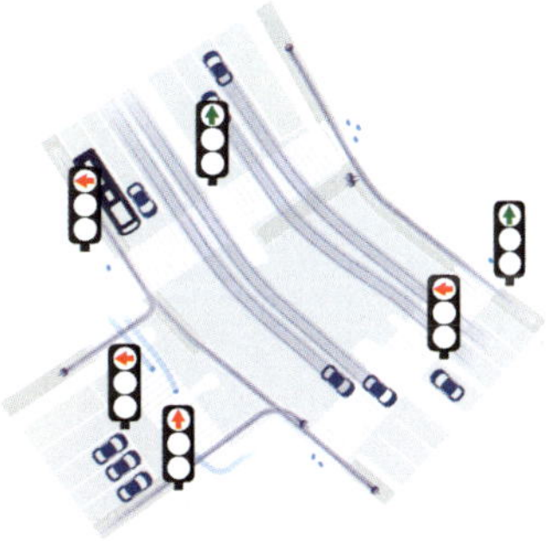

Phase 1

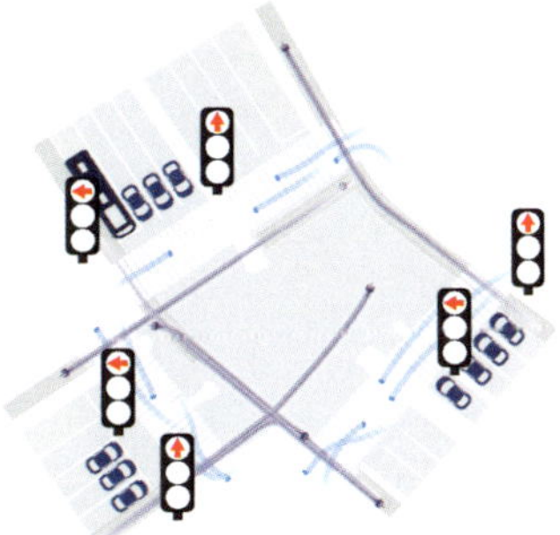

Phase 2

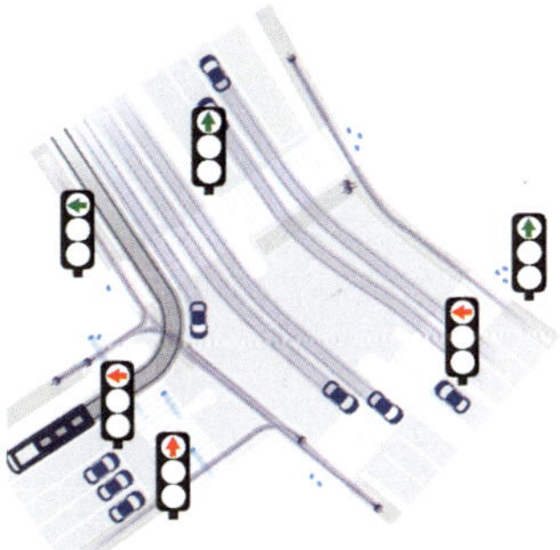

Phase 3

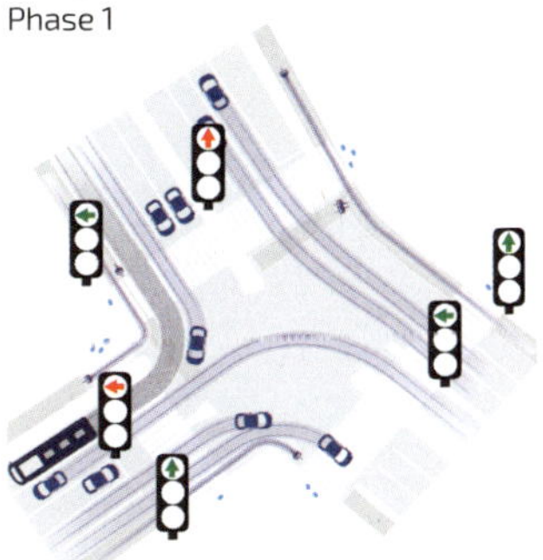

Phase 4

2. The intersection provides a time for pedestrian, bicycle and vehicle modes and for all crossings. The signal sequencing allows for all movements by limiting pedestrian/bicycle/vehicle crossings, but the combinatorics assures the crossing of as few movements as possible. There is a combination of alternating crossings.

Inner discipline to coexist with the crowd

Attractors and attractions
Offering multiple services for the daily needs of residents, Shibuya Square can accommodate up to several thousand people at a time. As such, it is the busiest pedestrian crossing in the world. It is an icon of Japanese tourism.

Modes
Pedestrians are in the majority (80%), far ahead of bicycles and vehicles. As a result, priority is given to pedestrians.

Activities
The peak hour is usually in the evening when people leave their offices. Early in the morning, when all the shops and restaurants are closed, there are fewer pedestrians. The traffic is linked to that of the nearby Shibuya Station.

Modal share

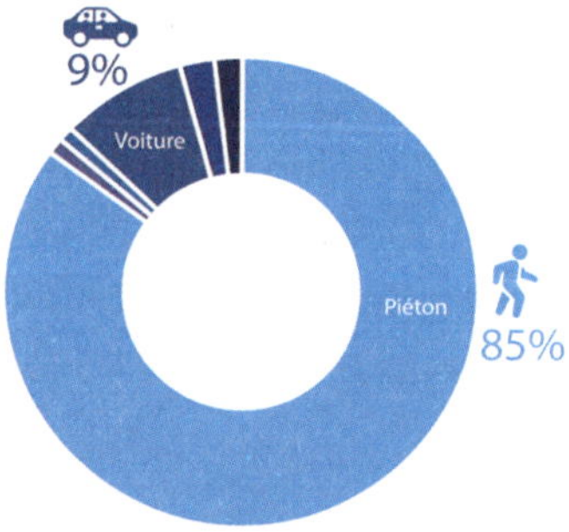

Elements in movement

730/3mn

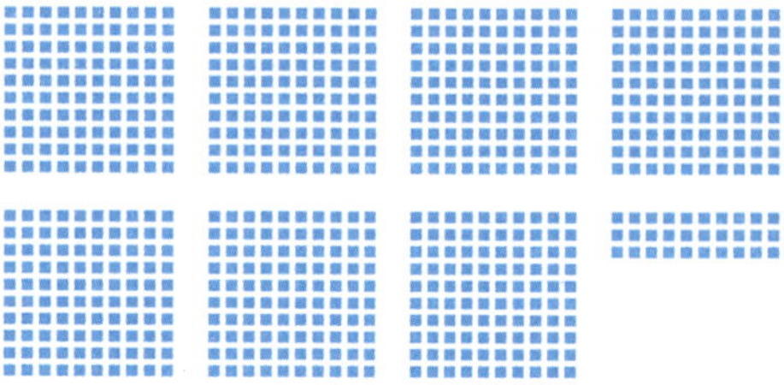

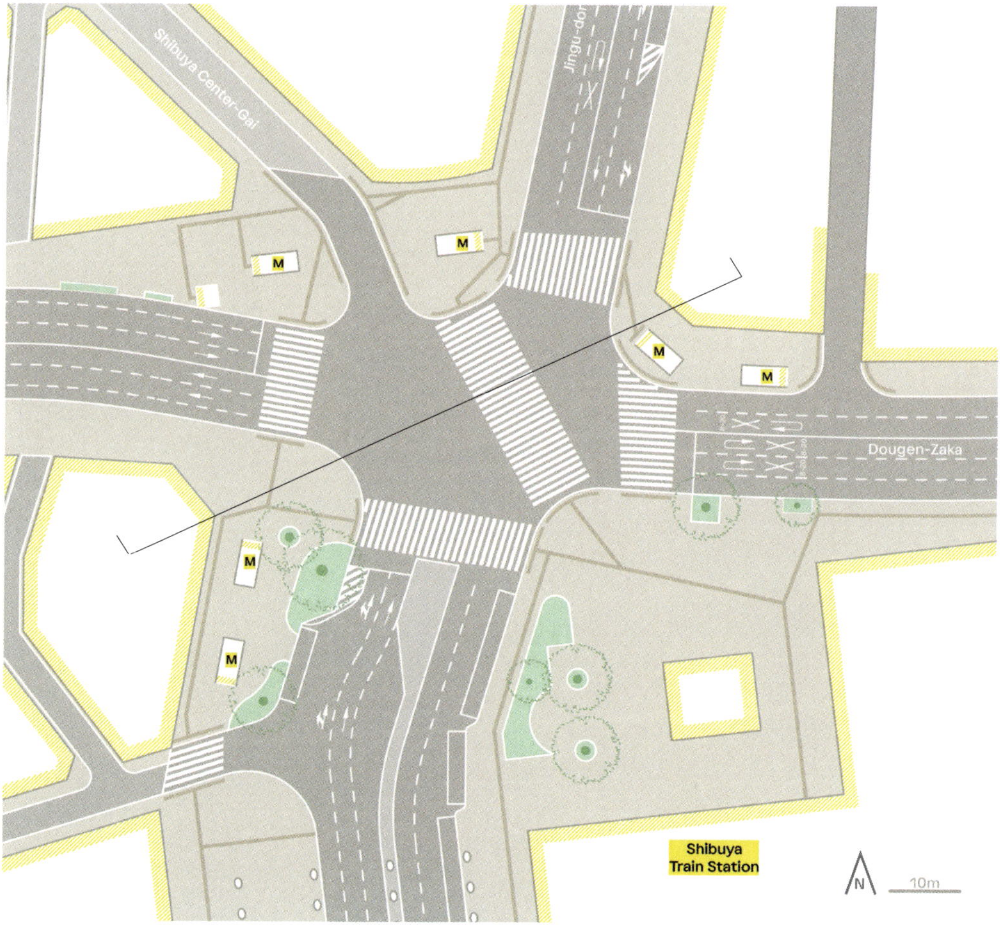

support

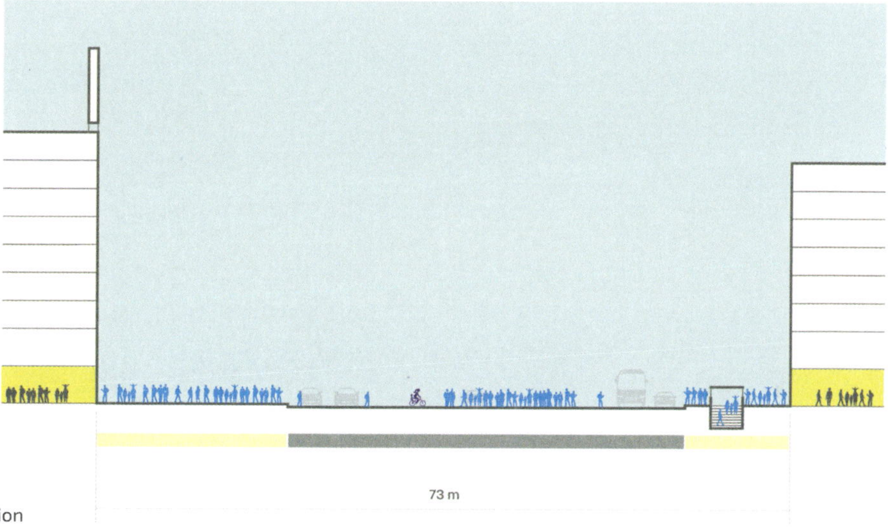

elevation

3-phase regularizatio

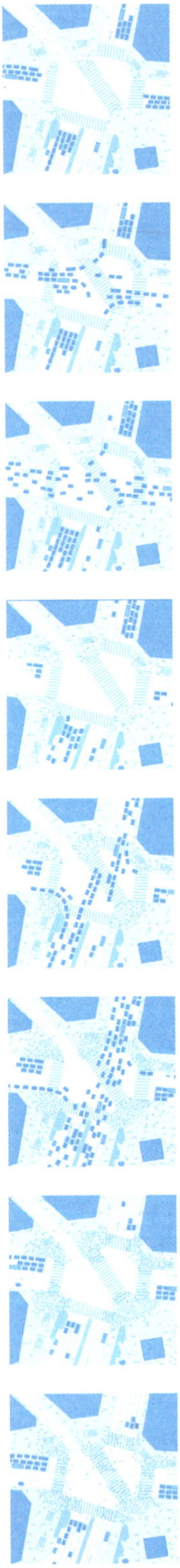

Attendance over a period of 3 minutes

MINIMUM ACTIVITY
05H00

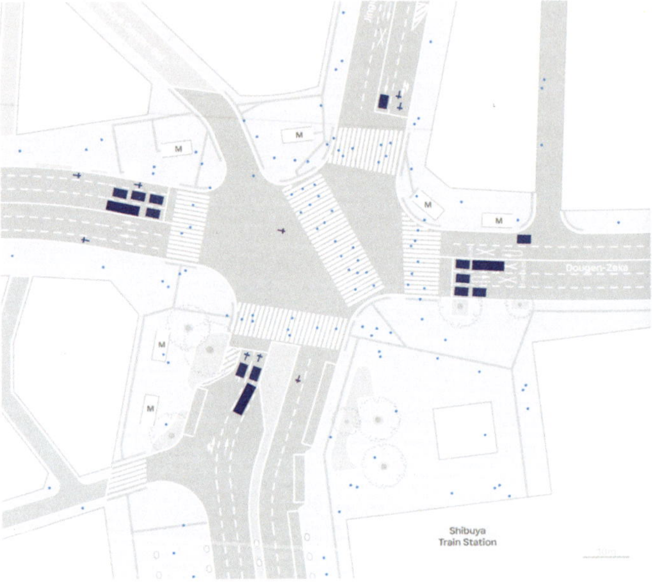

Bus · Truck · Car · Bike · Electric rickshaw · Rickshaw · Bicycle · Rollerblading, skateboarding and scootering · Pedestrian · Animal · Mobile stationary

MAXIMUM ACTIVITY
17H00

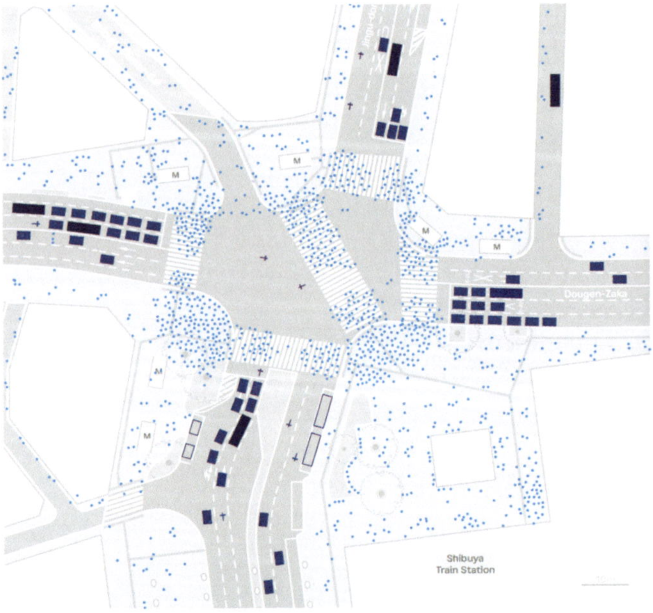

and following the codes

Variations of movements

The movement of vehicles is fast and continuous because the alternating crossings are respected and clear. The traffic lights are three-stage, with a specific phase for pedestrians allowing diagonal crossing. Car traffic is on the left side of the lanes.

Every 80 seconds, when the movement of vehicles stops, the orderly streets of Shibuya are transformed with the movement of pedestrians in all directions and everywhere. Pedestrians spread out across the width of the intersection to avoid oncoming traffic and make it easier to cross. The view is quite chaotic because movements take place in all directions, with the flexibility of pedestrian movements. This said, pedestrians strictly follow the timing of the lights and wait in line on the sidewalk to cross. Pedestrians take advantage of the last moment to cross thanks to a displayed timer.

Pedestrian movements are organic flows in all directions.

Traffic goes in both directions on the lanes. Vehicles often stop to give way to the opposite side and maneuver the vehicle in the overtaking direction.

Bicycle users can use the vehicle lanes, but they also ride on the sidewalks. Cyclists ride on the left side of the road. When crossing the intersection, cyclists can join pedestrians, but they get off their bikes.

One-way turns and U-turns are absent.

Tactics of movements diagrams

The movement here is a combination of strict movements, those of the vehicles, and organic movements, those of the pedestrians. The fast-paced pedestrians create a swarming atmosphere with very flexible trajectories.

Time 1

Time 2

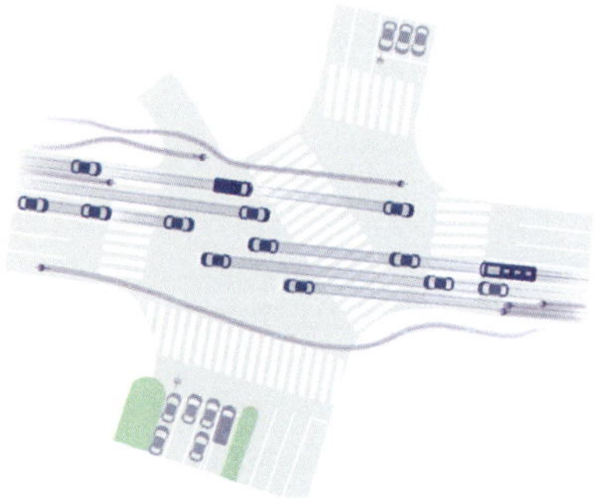

1. Time 1 is very different from Time 2 in terms of movements. Bicycles are found among pedestrians and vehicles. There are no dedicated bike lanes.

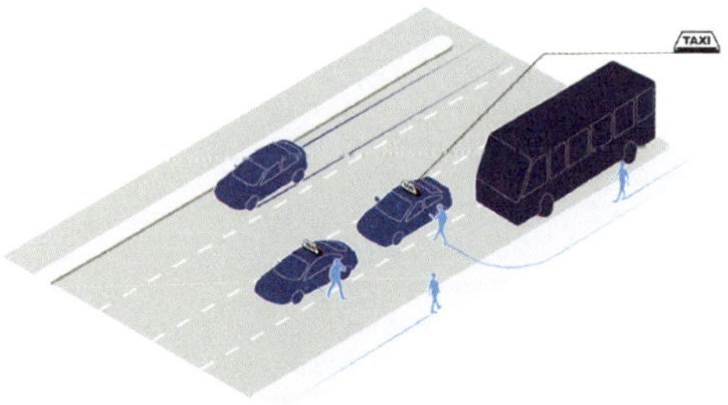

2. Taxis stop in the middle of the lane so as not to impede the passage of the bus.

Intersection
Dong Kinh Nghia Thuc Square

Continuous and vital movement

Attractors and attractions

The shops and restaurants are the main attractors of the area, with a high number of visitors. The square is one of the city's main attractions. The clothing market and leisure activities, with the lake and the fountain in the centre, also operate during the night, wich further enhances the continuous use of the site.

Modes

Motorcycles are the most common mode of travel because they are fast, easy to maneuver and to park. They usually ride on the left side of the street. The modal split therefore shows a strong majority of small vehicles (motorcycles) and pedestrians.

Activities

The busiest time is at night because the thriving night market attracts many pedestrians. Early in the morning, the intersection is quieter, when only the hotels are in operation. During the day, ice cream vendors set up shop near the lake. The shops often spread their goods on the sidewalks, leaving narrow passages for pedestrians. The anarchic parking of motorcycles is also a common practice on the sidewalks and roads.

Modal share

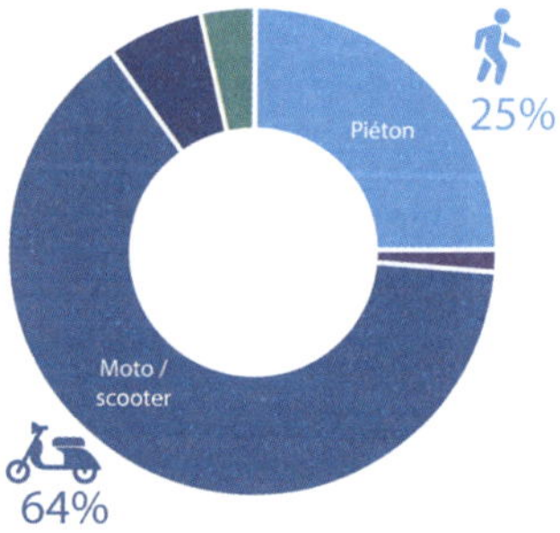

Elements in movement

420/3mn

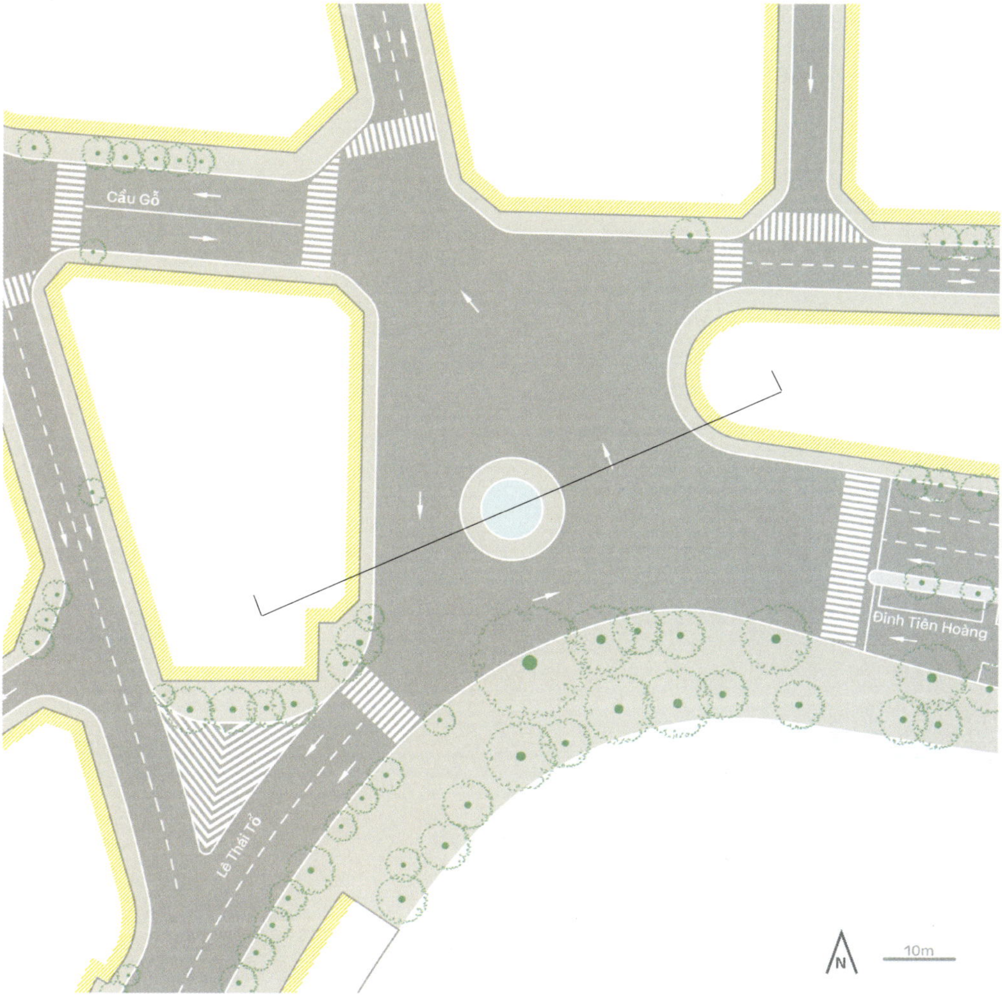

support

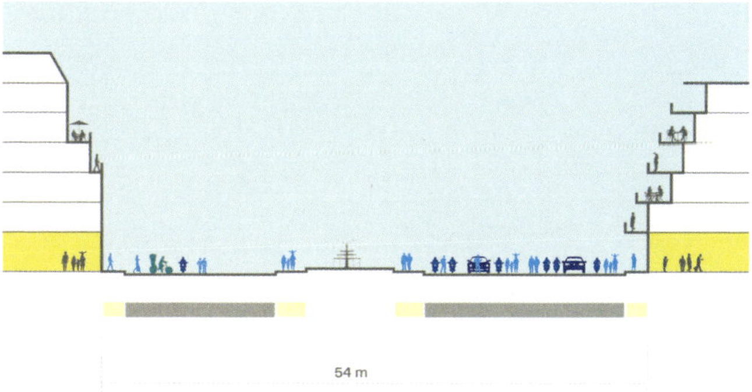

elevation

Small roundabout

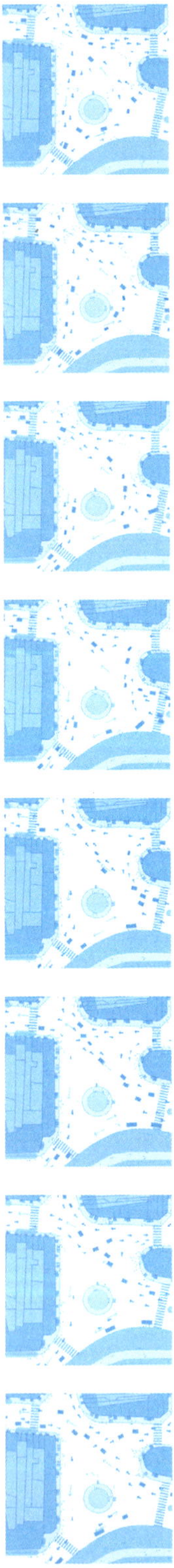

Attendance over a period of 3 minutes

MINIMUM ACTIVITY
05H00

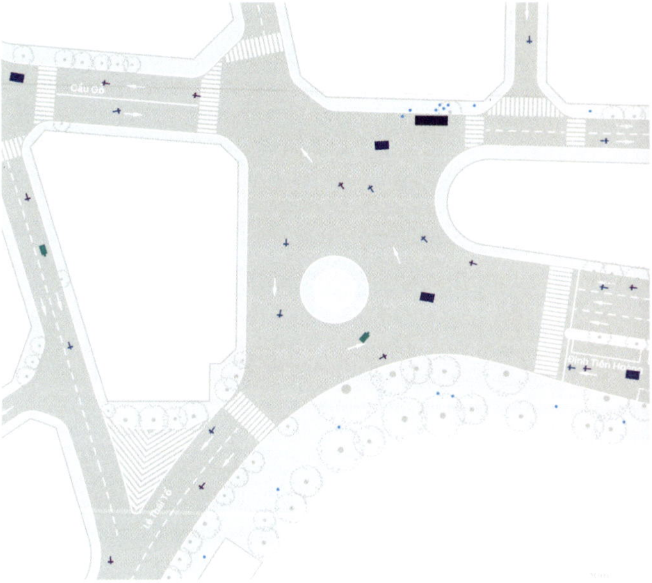

Bus
Truck
Car
Bike
Electric rickshaw
Rickshaw
Bicycle
Rollerblading, skateboarding and scootering
Pedestrian
Animal
Mobile stationary

MAXIMUM ACTIVITY
20H00

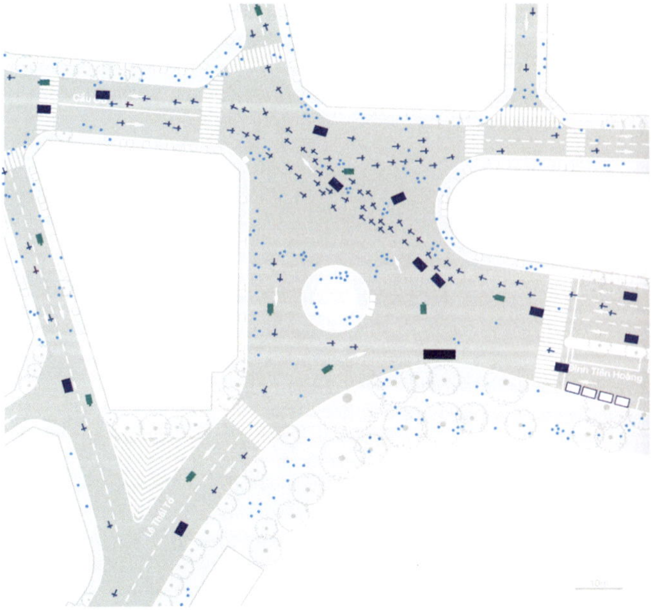

and slow speed for all

Variations of movements

Pedestrians move more quickly along the sidewalks, in the lane. They slow down and detour at crossroads.

Pedestrians often occupy the road and leave the crossings reserved for them. Crossing freely is a common phenomenon.

The movement of vehicles is slow and continuous.

Vietnamese will habitually deviate a little from their trajectory, instead of stopping to cross another mobile element.

The traffic of motor vehicles is fluid and noisy, because the driver often indicates to the other mobile elements not to modify their trajectory by honking and then deviates his/her trajectory to avoid them, responding to the regularity of their movement. Thus pedestrians move slowly and above all with regular speed in the streets, in the middle of vehicles that do not stop.

Most streets have defined movement patterns, but disobeying traffic rules is common. A driver must be vigilant because a mobile element can come from any direction.

Some of the stationary merchants are located on the busy lanes and impede circulation.

The intersection is organized around a small fountain, without traffic lights. The movement is continuous and irregular. Some people are near the fountain in the center of the intersection.

Tactics of movements diagrams

The movement of the mobile elements appears very free but very slow, without signs of impatience despite honking. Thanks to the slowness, the diversity of the flows appears as a global fluid movement.

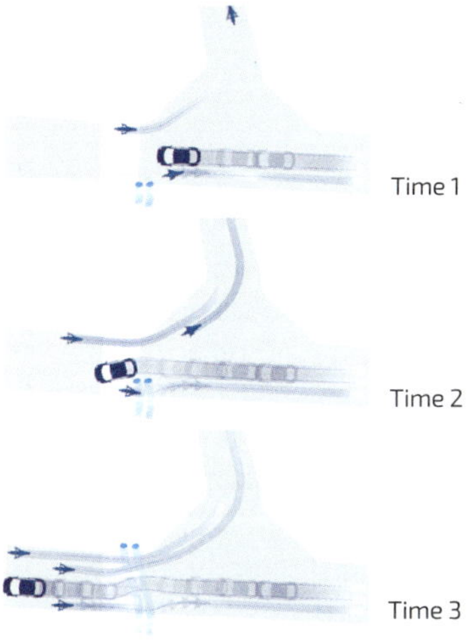

1. The very low speed at the crossing and the fluid negotiation of the crossing between the mobile elements allows to avoid stops.

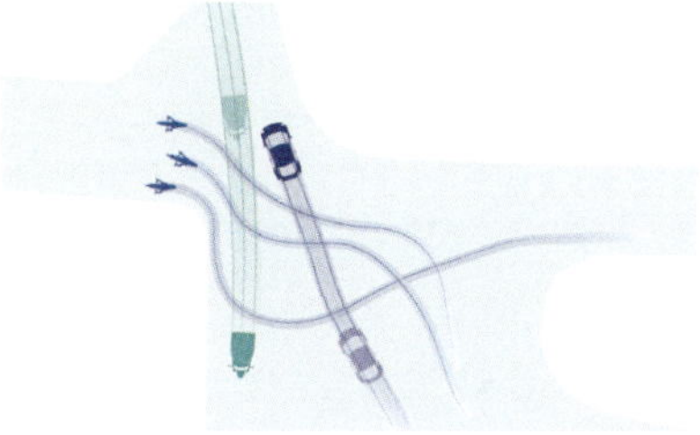

2. We observe the formation of small groups of vehicles going in the same direction and facilitating their crossing with a "mass effect" for the single vehicle arriving in front.

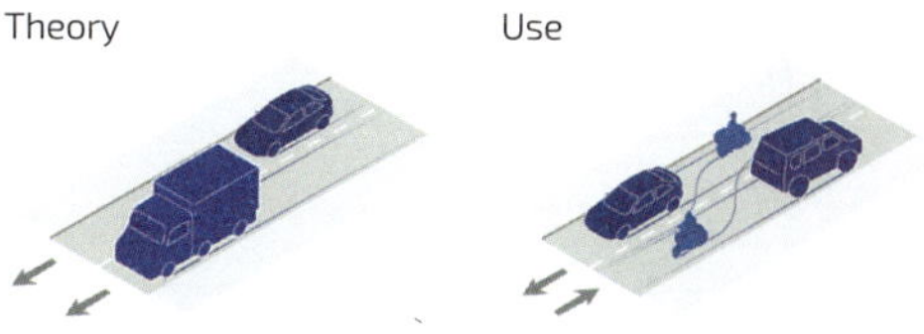

3. The lanes that are theoretically one-way are actually used by motorized two-wheelers in both directions, and sometimes by cars.

Oxford Circus Intersection
Oxford Street and Regent Street

Contraction of roads and a time for each mode

Attractors and attractions

The shops and the metro station generate a lot of pedestrian traffic. There are many recreational facilities (monuments, bars, gardens) nearby.

Modes

The double-decker buses run with high frequency and throughout the night. They are used extensively. The strong presence of shops and the central location of the district explain the presence of many pedestrians wich is 3 times larger than that of cars.

Activities

Traffic is highest in the evening when people go to bars and shops after office hours. There is little movement at night after the shops and public transport have closed.

Modal share

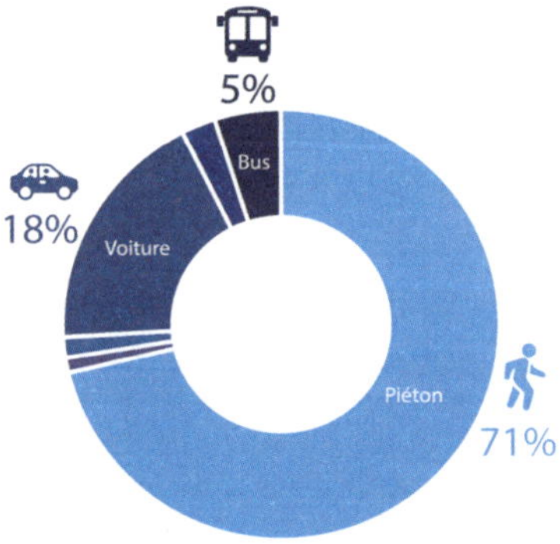

Elements in movement

460/3mn

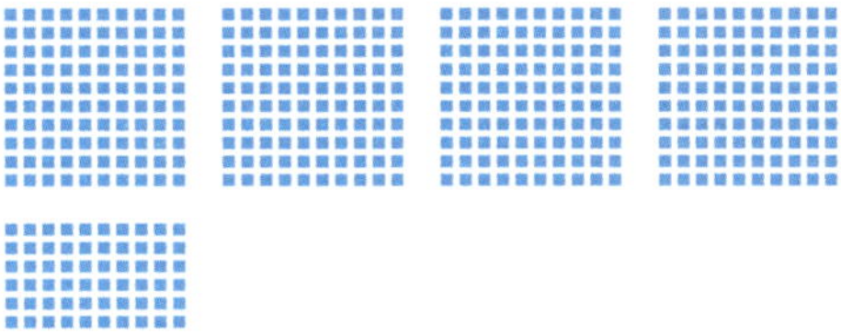

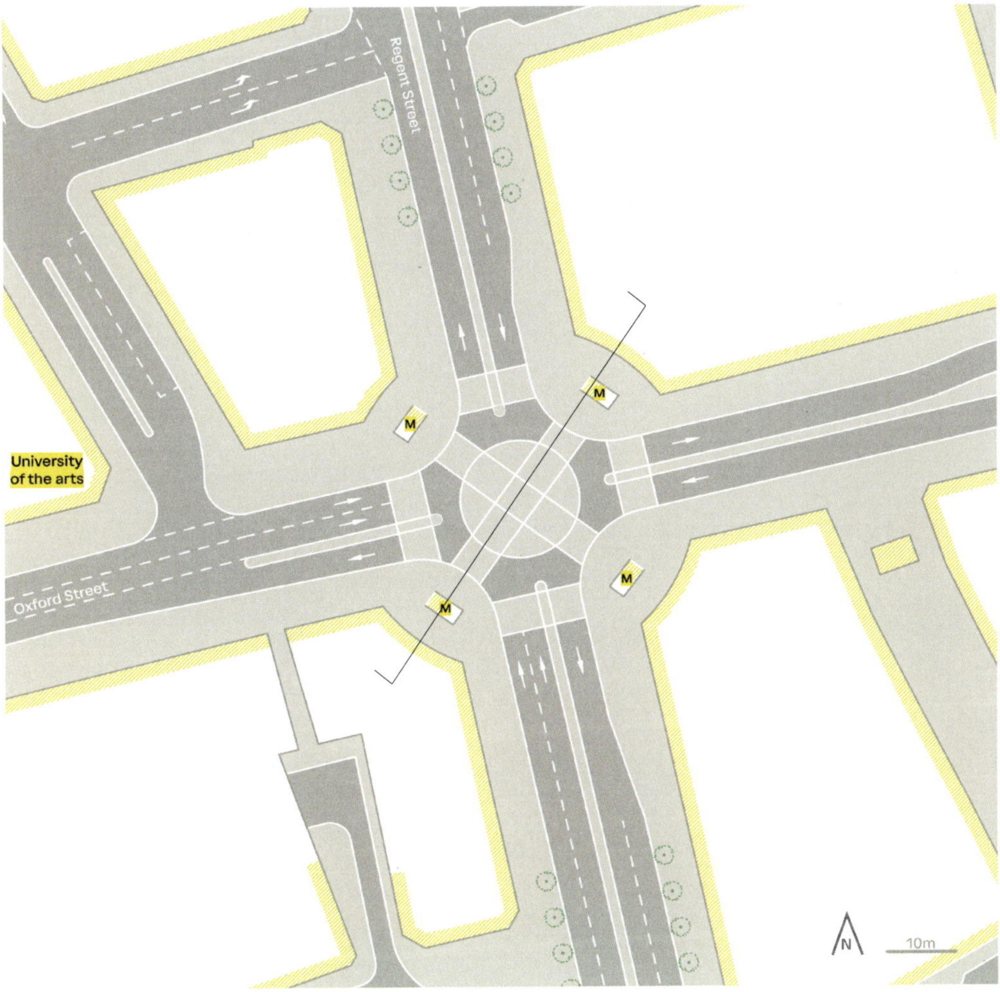

support

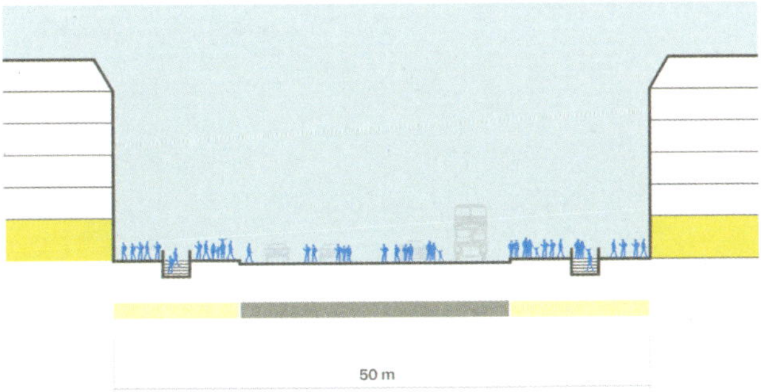

elevation

3-phase regulation

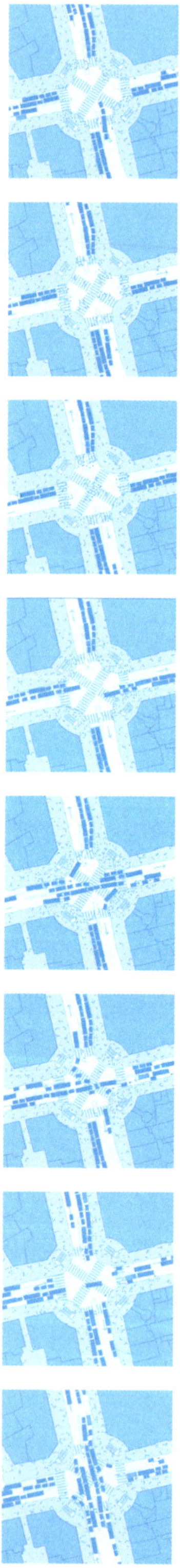

Attendance over a period of 3 minutes

MINIMUM ACTIVITY
05H00

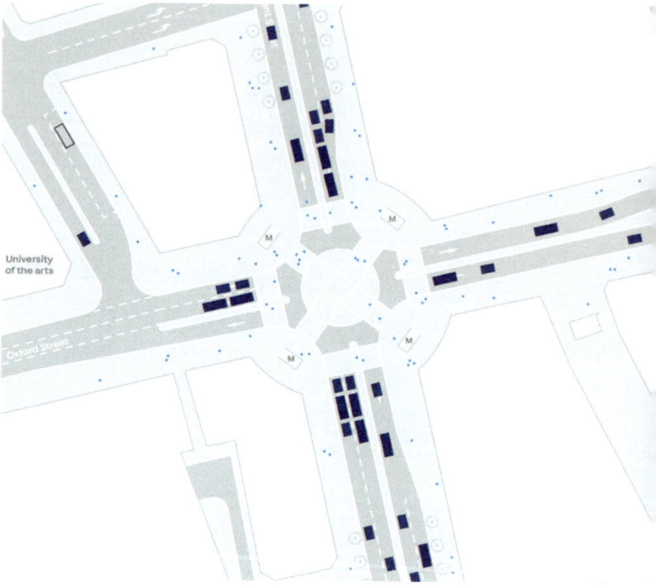

Bus
Truck
Car
Bike
Electric rickshaw
Rickshaw
Bicycle
Rollerblading, skateboarding and scootering
Pedestrian
Animal
Mobile stationary

MAXIMUM ACTIVITY
18H00

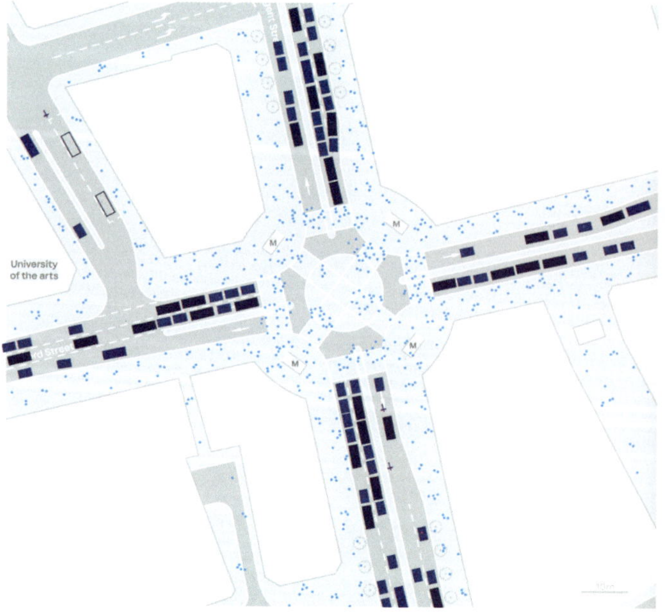

Variations of movements

The roadways in the intersection are limited to 2 lanes and sometimes one of them is reserved for buses. This limits speed and movement. Few bicycles are seen. Currently, they ride on the roadway. The "right turn" movement is not set up. Vehicles wait in the middle of the intersection, then turn. This movement takes place when the traffic lights turn yellow.

The presence of wide medians in the middle of the lanes allows pedestrians to stop in the middle when crossing. Thus, pedestrians can cross at red lights, when there are no cars, by taking refuge on the medians. Two attitudes are then possible: the classic and slower one, by waiting for the red light, and the more hurried one, by crossing quickly in two steps, by slipping between a micro-interruption of the vehicle traffic.

The intersection is equipped with three-stage traffic lights to allow diagonal pedestrian crossing. This brings car traffic to a complete halt and allows pedestrians to cross exclusively in all directions.

Tactics of movements diagrams

Pedestrian traffic has the priority, and the sidewalks are as wide as the car and bus lanes. Pedestrian traffic is very free compared to the very constrained vehicle traffic.

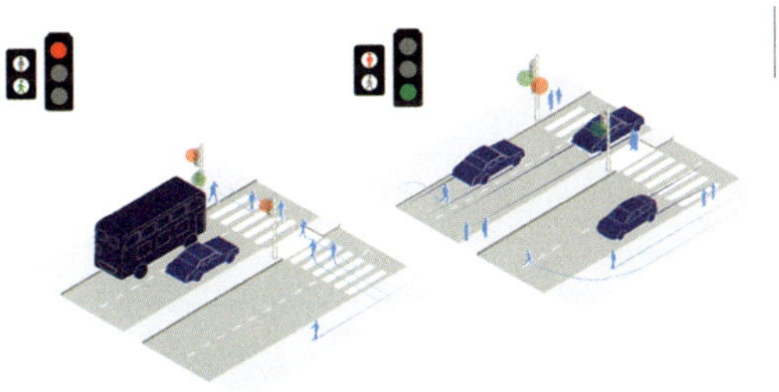

When the light is green for pedestrians, crossing is done in one go on the crosswalks. When the traffic light is red for pedestrians, many wait and some run to the medians to cross more quickly, in two steps, as soon as there are no vehicles.

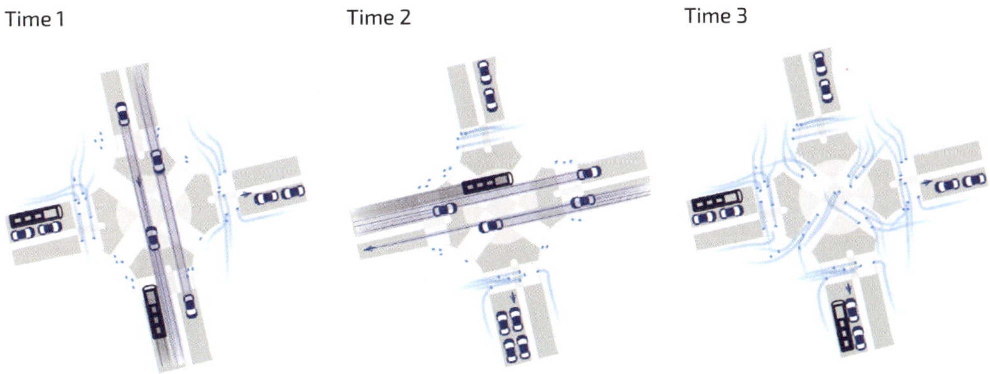

The design of the intersections gives an important place to pedestrians with wide sidewalks and a specific time at red lights for crossing the intersection in all directions.

Intersection Ojuelegba Road, Alagbede-Igbobi Road and A1 Highway

Moving with saturation and exchanges

Attractors and attractions
Many bus stops are present, which makes this intersection an important passing place of the capital. itinerant shops are set up around the bus stops. The programs around the square bring together shops and workshops. All these activities and the traffic jams make the intersection attractive for the local street vendors.

Modes
The majority of vehicles are public transport vehicles, mini-buses (yellow) or motorcycles. There are also many pedestrians. Cars are present in the intersection and mainly on the viaduct. The modal split is very diverse.

Activities
Rush hour is the end of the workday when people are heading home. This can be identified on the highways with traffic jams. Days in Lagos start early, so the streets are rarely empty.

Modal share

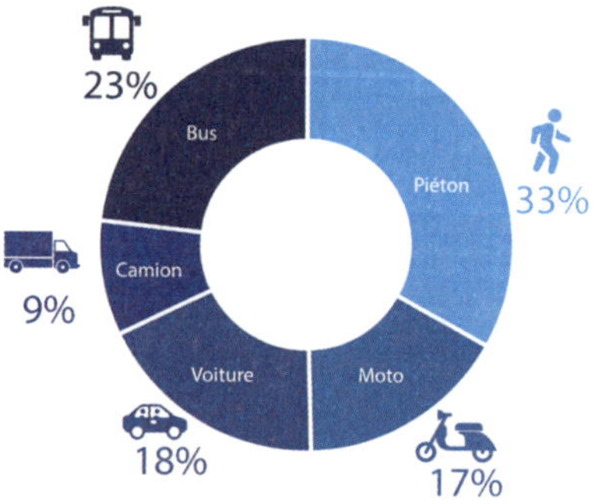

Elements in movement

240/3mn

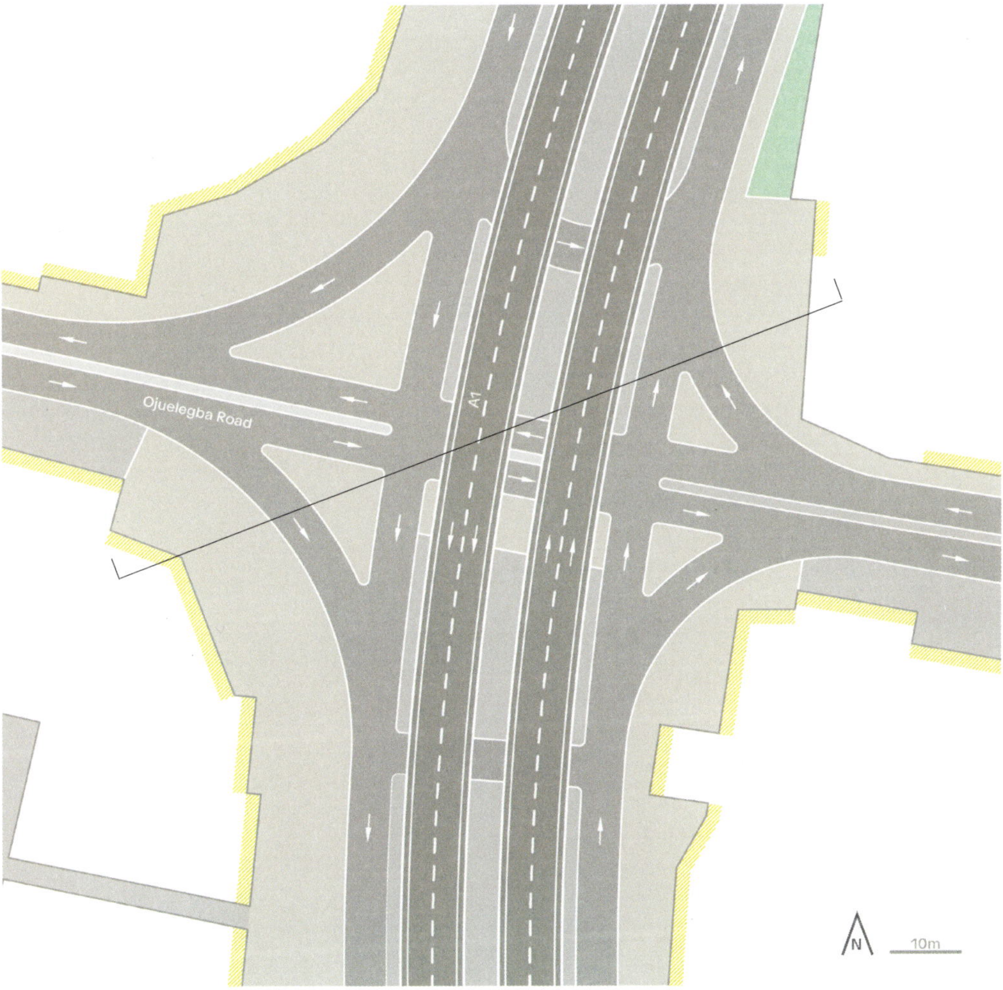

support

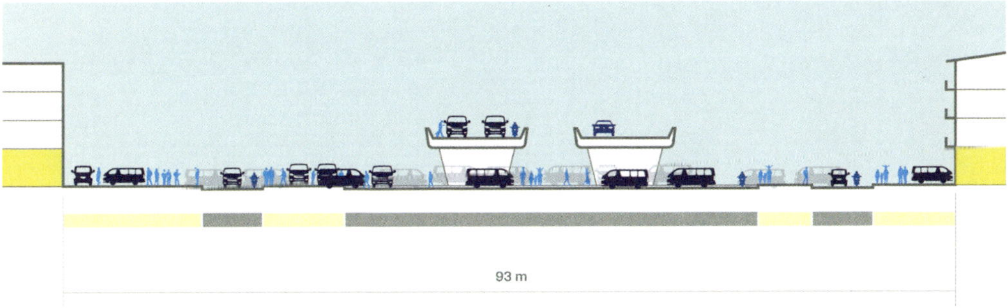

elevation

Regulation, separatio

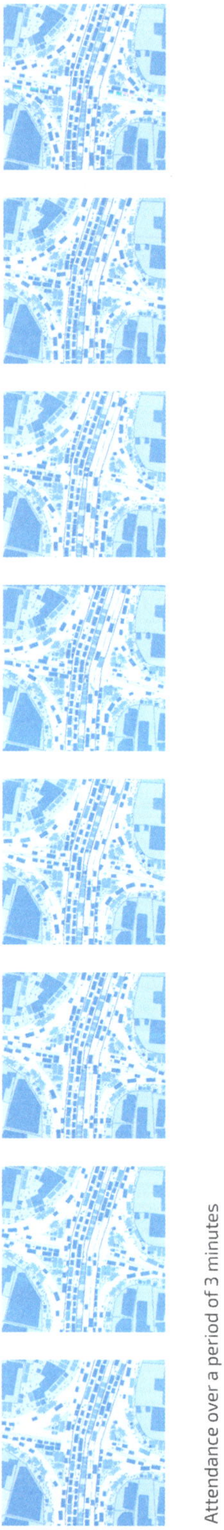

MINIMUM ACTIVITY
04H00

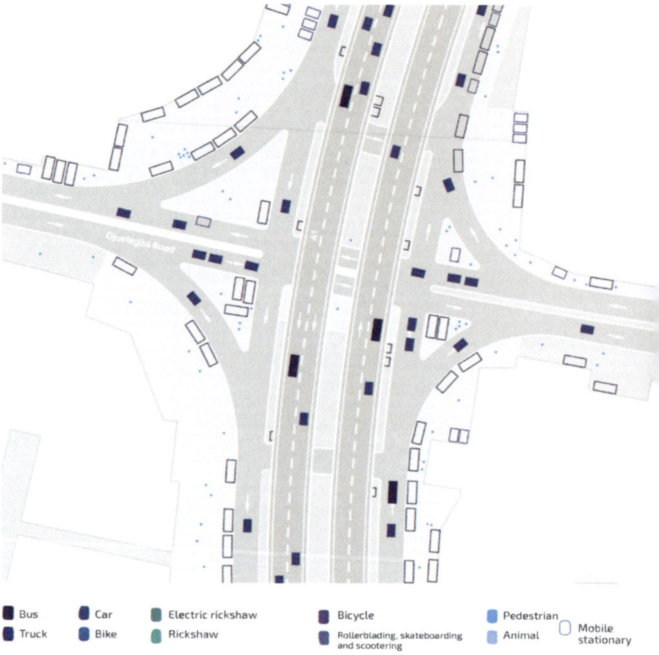

MAXIMUM ACTIVITY
18H00

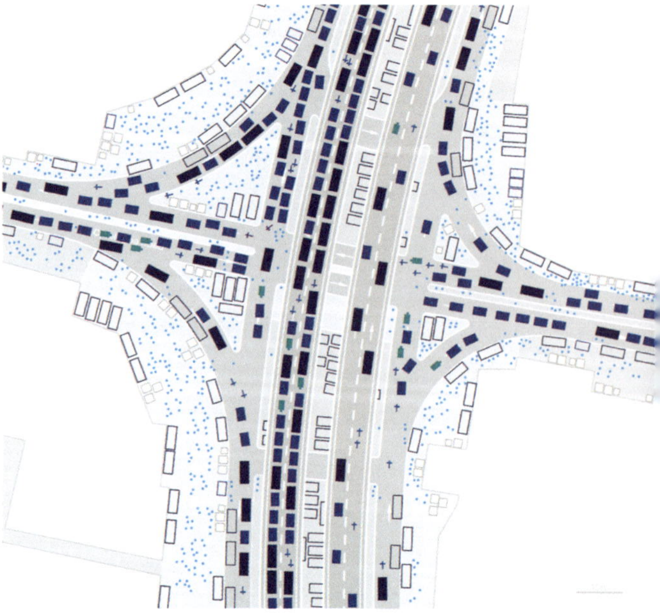

saturation and stops

Variations of movemens

The roads carry more vehicles than they can handle, and behavior is very anarchic, leading to traffic jams. All this increases driver impatience, resulting in horns blowing and insistent headlight flashes.

As the cars remain stuck in traffic for a long time, peddlers on foot approach the vehicles to sell and thus turn the roads into a market.

Minibuses looking for customers park around the intersection, without predefined locations. Many buses stop in the middle of the roads.

Vehicle movements are unstable, sometimes very fast, sometimes slow and sometimes sudden, due to the unexpected arrival of other mobile elements.

Pedestrian movements are unpredictable, and most people cross in a random and unpredictable way. Most sidewalks are congested, often leading to people walking on the roads.

The intersection separates the directions of vehicular traffic for "right turns" and is equipped with traffic lights. The crossings are at the same level, except for the motorway overpass. Thus, the crossing areas are numerous and tightly packed with temporary occupancies everywhere.

Tactics of movements diagrams

The high level of traffic at the intersection causes regular and lengthy congestion. There is lots of activity and gathering.

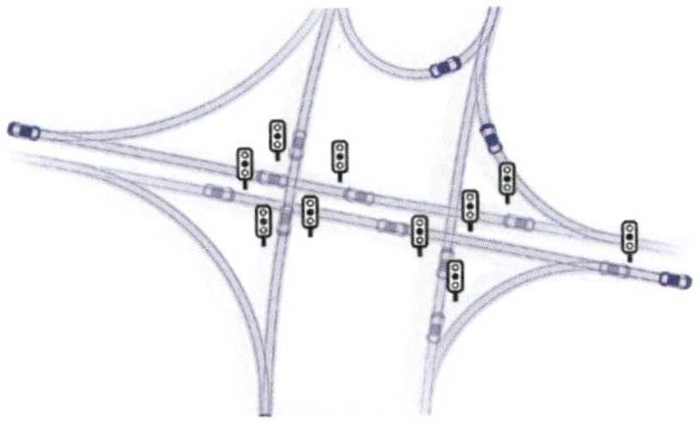

1. Traffic movements are separated by islands to distinguish between the directions of traffic. Crossings are at the same level and managed by traffic lights.

Time 1

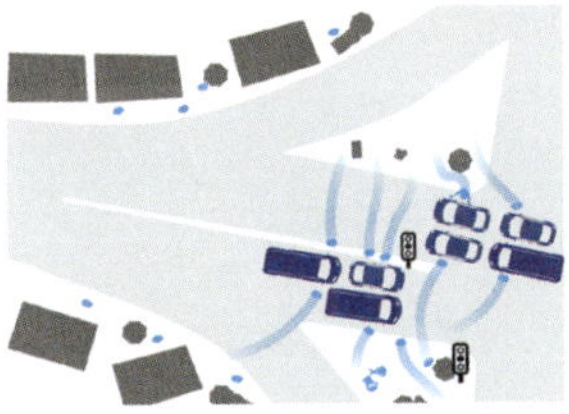

Time 2

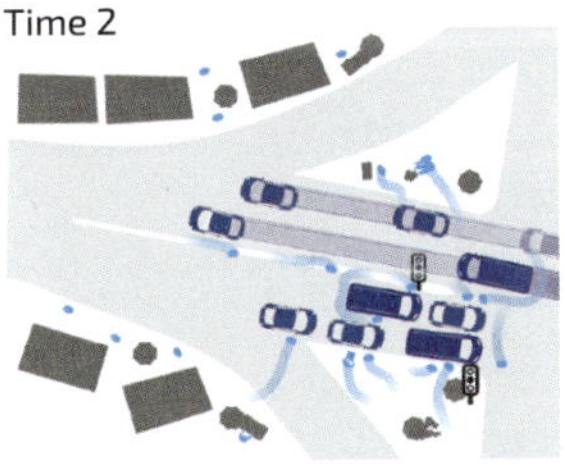

Time 3

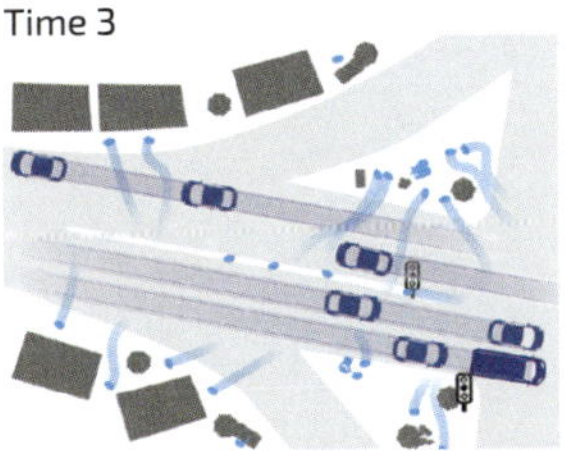

2. The concentration of peddlers is high around the vehicles because of their long stops on the roads. Waiting times are very long, unrelated to the two minutes of conventional traffic lights, either on the roads or on the highway overpass.

Intersection Av. Brigadeiro g Faria Lima and Av. President Juscelino Kubitschek

Prohibited directions and waiting for speed

Attractors and attractions
The nearby restaurants, hotels and banks act as important polarities in this office district.

Modes
Traffic is mainly car traffic, with the recent inclusion of bicycles. Pedestrians and motorcycles are also present, but in a minority (3 times less). There is little bus traffic in the intersection

Activities
Traffic is highest in the early evening, just after the end of office hours, and can last well into the night. There is less traffic in the early morning, but the site is generally busy all day.

Modal share

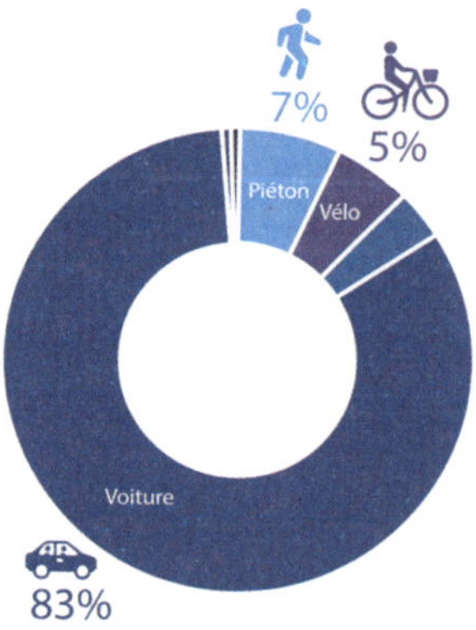

Elements in movement

510/3mn

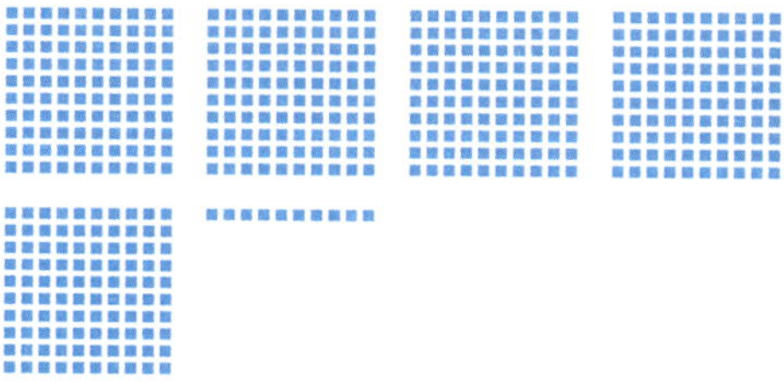

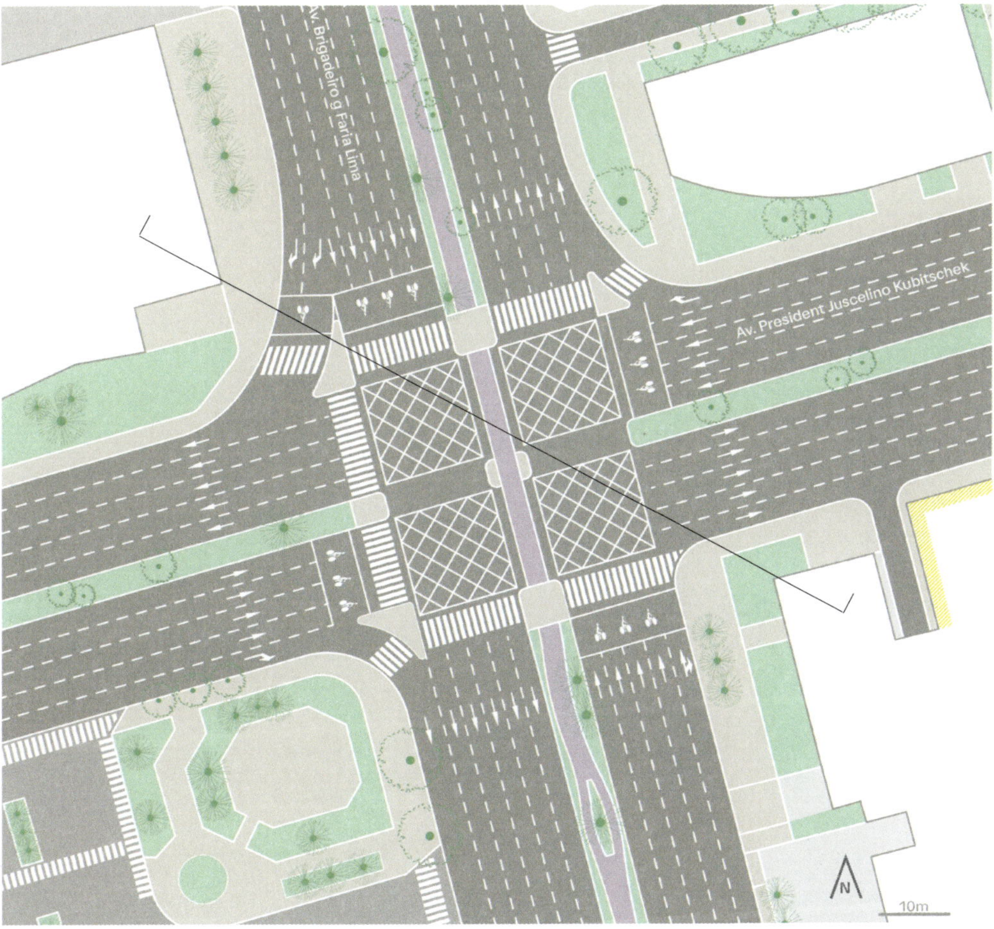

support

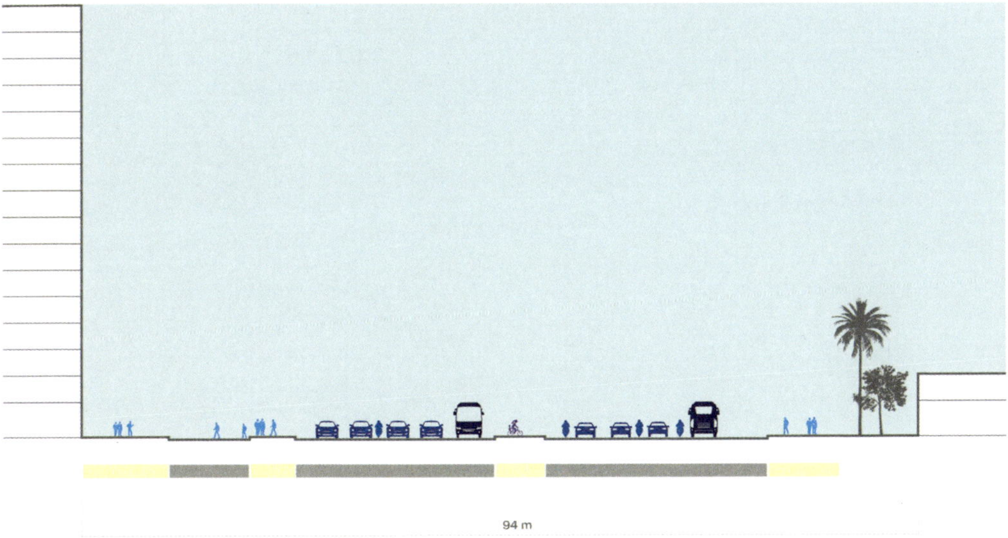

elevation

Intersection Av. Brigadeiro g Faria Lima and Av. President Juscelino Kubitschek

Attendance over a period of 3 minutes

2-phase regulation

MINIMUM ACTIVITY
06H00

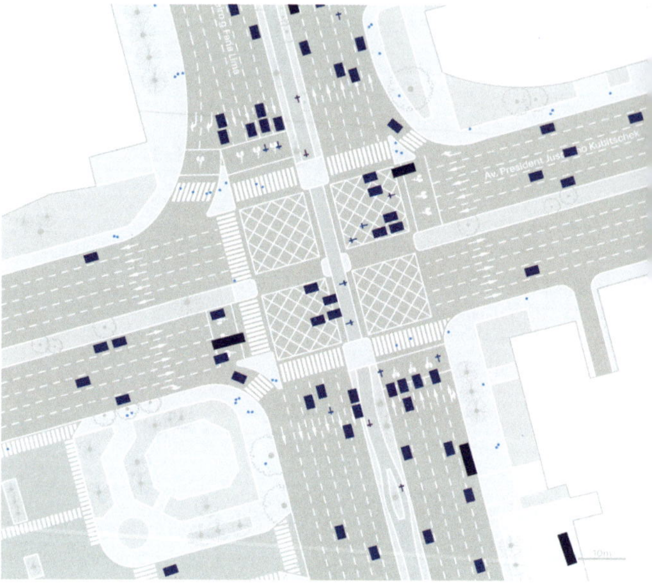

MAXIMUM ACTIVITY
17H00

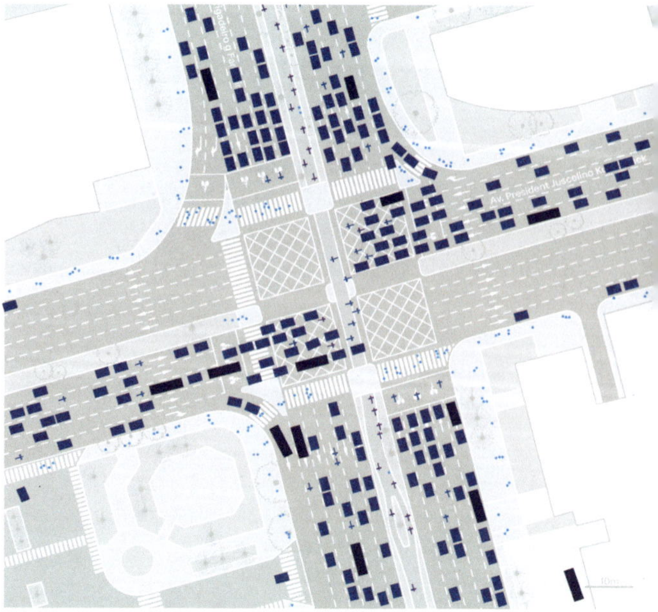

Variations of movements

Recently, a separate lane was built for bicycles and pedestrians. This bicycle lane is axial, creating a separation of the traffic directions. Nevertheless, the "left turn" for bicycles remains difficult, as they have to stop to let cars pass and wait for the light to change color.

All right-turn movements wait a long time for the traffic lights, even if special lanes are provided.

Cyclists often stop next to the pedestrian crossing to change direction. Most pedestrians walk within the crosswalk, only a few pedestrians walk in the gaps between the bike path and the vehicle road in the middle of the lane.

Cars follow the rules of the traffic and respect the lanes. They move quickly, without obstruction and follow the regulations. For those who want to go even faster, like motorcyclists, they move from one lane to another, without respecting the speed limit and overtaking on the left.

Intersections are unsafe due to the common practice of carjacking. As a result, vehicles tend to skip traffic light stops at night when there is not much traffic.

The intersection has two-stage traffic signals on a "checkerboard" pattern, with no direct "left turns" for cars. This configuration limits crossings. It is also typical of the traffic pattern in cities in the United States.

Tactics of movements diagrams

The intensity and management of traffic in Sao Paulo appear restrictive: it is impossible to turn left and waiting times at traffic lights are long for all users. Alternative mobility tactics are rare and dangerous (cycling).

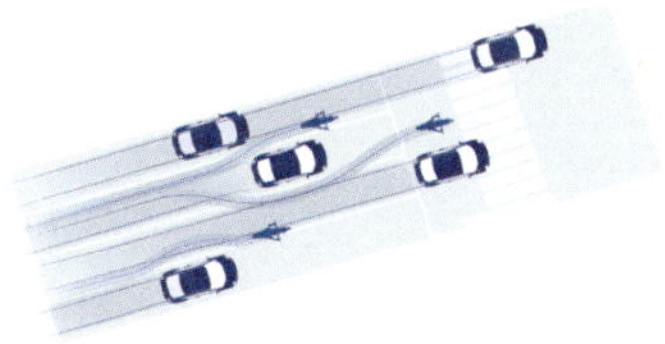

1. Motorcyclists break the rules of the road by overtaking on all sides.

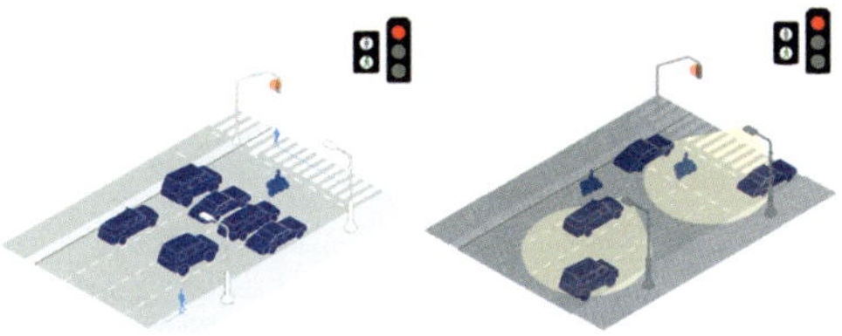

2. During the day, traffic lights are respected. At night, cars do not stop because of the risk of assault when stopped.

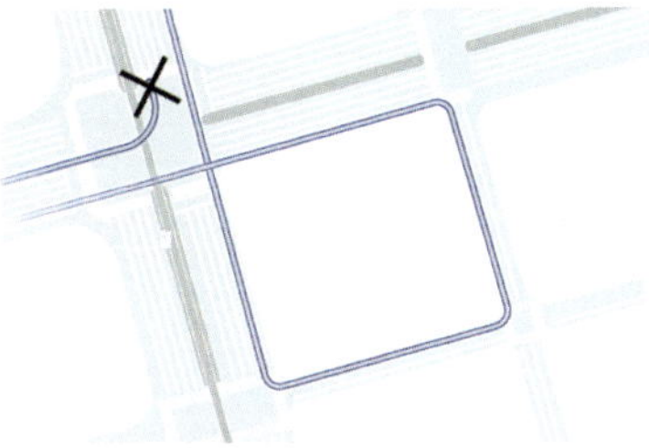

3. Vehicles do not turn left (crossing side), instead, three turns are required to do so, bypassing the private island ("the block").

4. Bicycles cross the intersection in the center for the north-south direction and laterally for the east-west direction, following the traffic lights.

Oversized lanes and an intersection to manage

Attractors and attractions
The intersection is located on the busy road leading to Wudaokou Station. Nearby libraries, shops and restaurants act as important attractors.

Modes
While the majority of mobile elements are cars, the presence of two-wheelers, pedestrians and trucks is significant.

Activities
The wide roads are designed to accommodate a maximum of traffic. However, they are overrun with cars, often causing blockages at the intersection. Nevertheless, all mobile elements have very flexible and free trajectories at the intersection.

Modal share

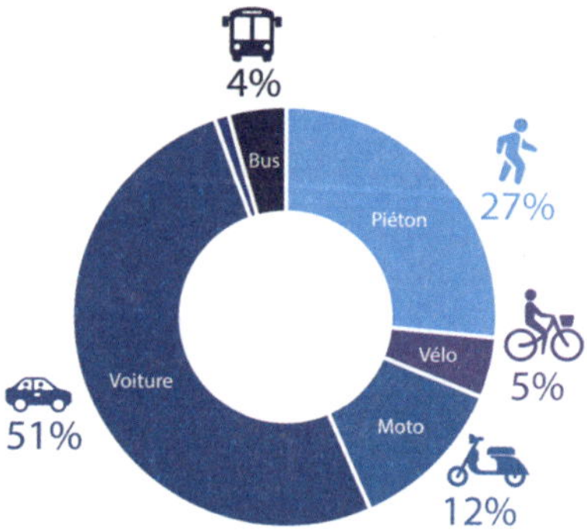

Elements in movement

650/3mn

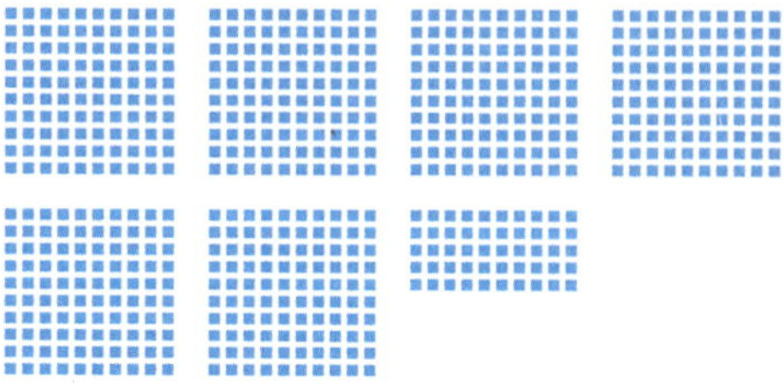

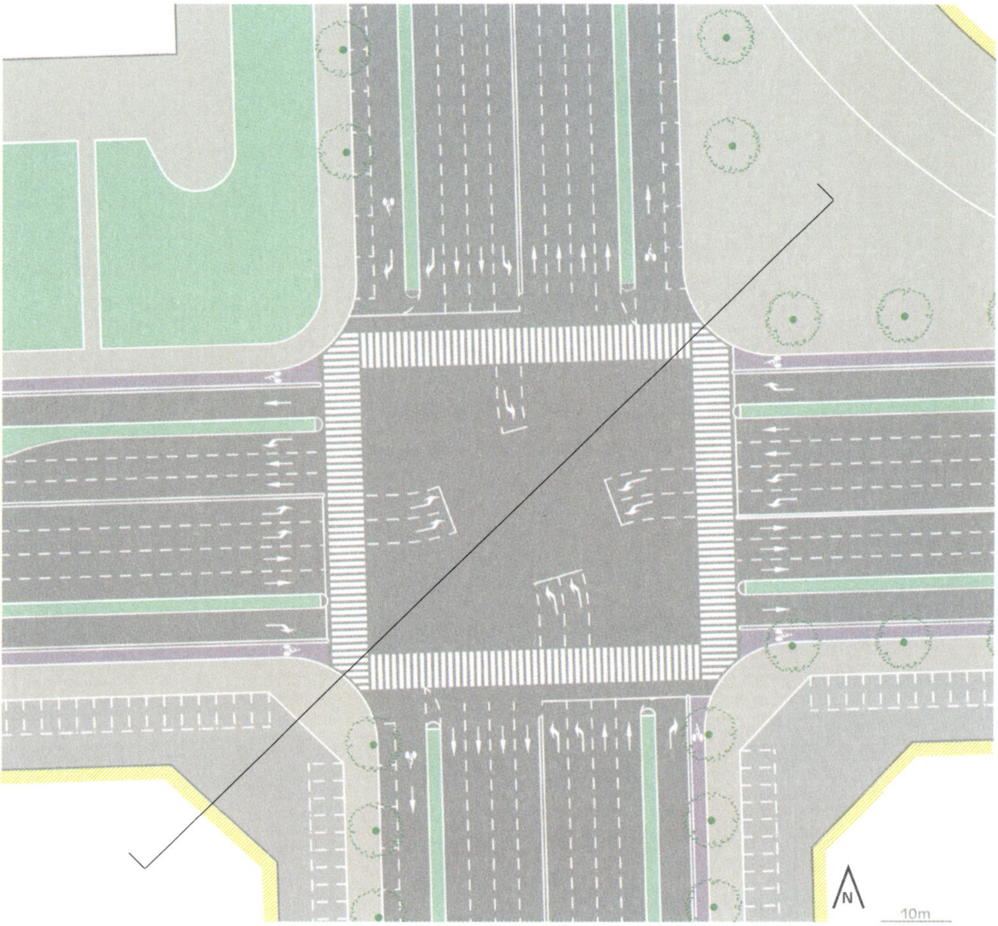

support

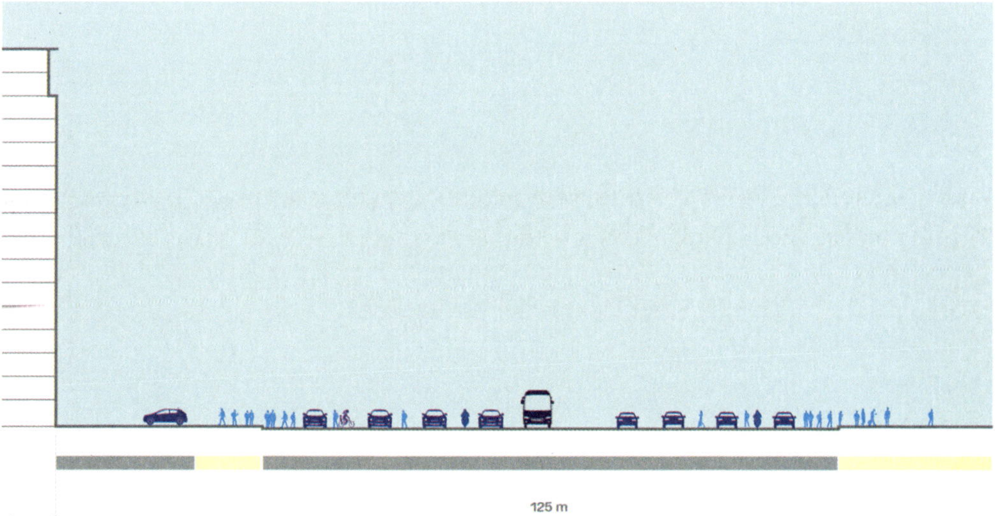

elevation

2-phase regulation

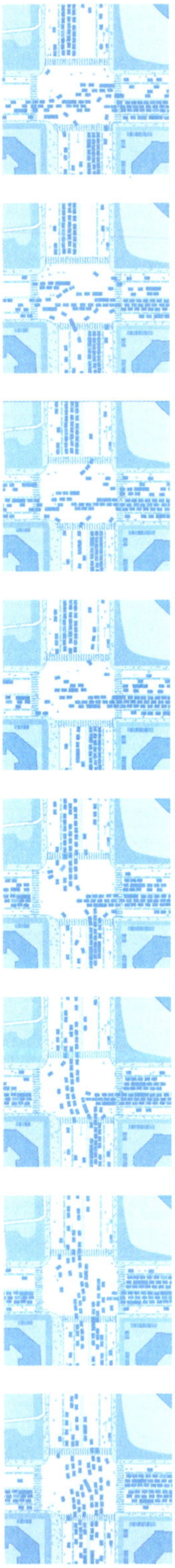

Attendance over a period of 3 minutes

MINIMUM ACTIVITY
06H00

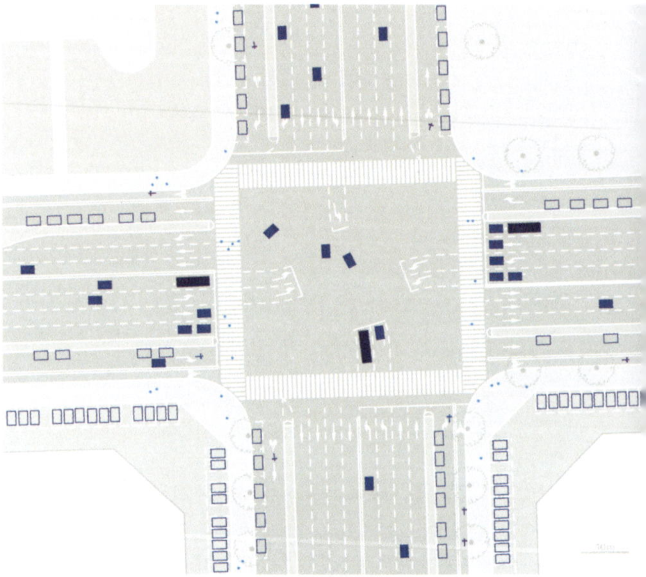

Bus
Truck
Car
Bike
Electric rickshaw
Rickshaw
Bicycle
Rollerblading, skateboarding and scootering
Pedestrian
Animal
Mobile stationary

MAXIMUM ACTIVITY
19H00

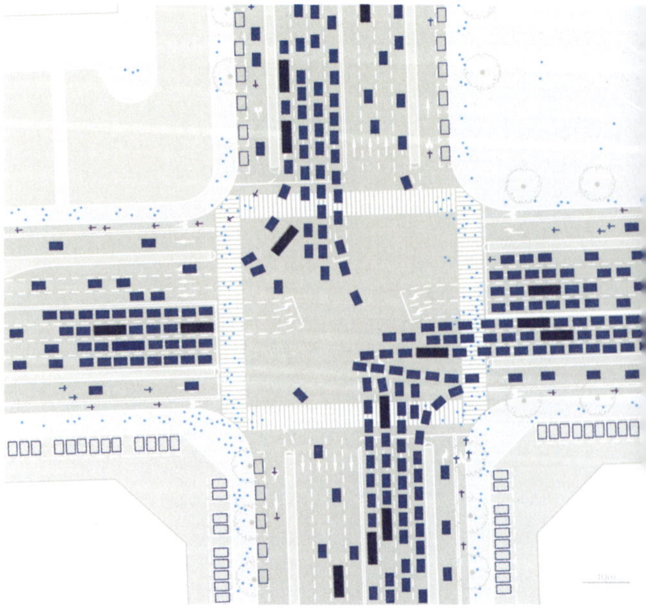

and service lanes

Variations of movements

Service lanes are located on either side of the traffic lanes, designed to facilitate "right turns" and entry into adjoining building plots. These lanes are primarily used by bicycles.

Slow traffic often annoys drivers who break traffic rules. Motorcycles and cyclists often disobey the rules and try to find ways to squeeze through and avoid the saturation of car traffic at the intersection.

Traffic light sequencing does not allow the flow of vehicles to drain completely at the intersection. This causes a traffic jam at the center, inhibiting the next movement and causing breaks in the flow. Some drivers take unauthorized routes on the side of the road.

Speeding vehicles frequently pass through the middle lanes, causing difficulties for vehicles intending to turn left.

Pedestrian flow is high, and pedestrians often use random routes to cross lanes, going wherever cars leave gaps. Thus, blocked cars honk frequently to claim the spaces taken over by pedestrians when they cross.

This is a traffic light intersection with side lanes and an "Indonesian-style" crossing principle, meaning that crossings take place in front of people and not behind as in Europe.

Tactics of movements diagrams

The response to the high traffic levels resulting from urbanization is to provide wide avenues. However, a high level of multi-modality and highly excessive traffic make passage of the crossings very hazardous.

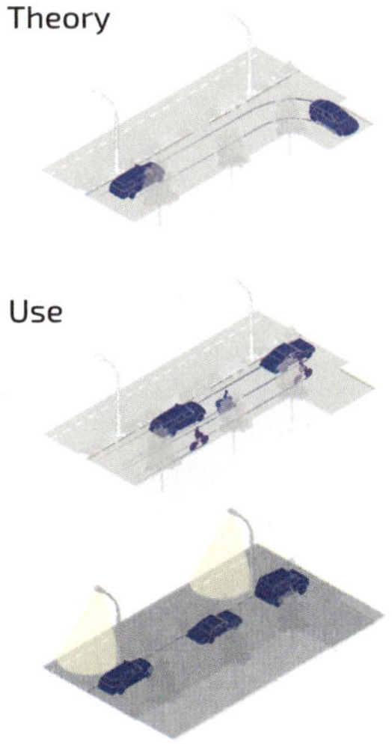

1. The side lanes change their use during the day. In normal traffic, they are used as a service road. In case of heavy traffic, two-wheelers use them to avoid the congested central lanes. At night, they are used as parking spaces.

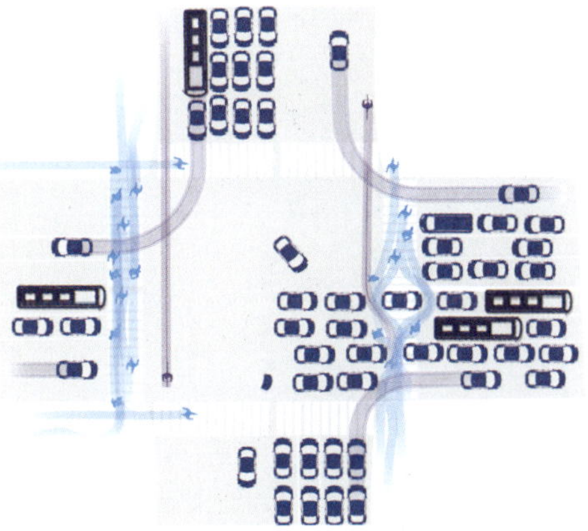

2. Passage at the crossing by cars is saturated. This blocks the next phase of the traffic light for the passage in the other direction. Pedestrians then take advantage of this to squeeze through the blocked cars.

ALDO
36-B1
202.86

III
MAIN POINTS IN MOVEMENTS TO CROSS PATHS

Our approach is based on the urban setting, mobile behavior and crossing devices. It is reflected in illustrations that combine this data. The representations of intersections since the beginning of the last century clearly show an analysis of the flow breakdown, the induced prioritization of modes, and even the disappearance of certain modes of travel according to the era.[21]

21 Alonzo, Eric, 2018, *L'architecture de la voie*. Histoire et théories. Marseille, Parenthèses.

Following the inclusive logic of urban spaces of exchange, the aim is instead to maintain the diversity and the possibility of movements together. We therefore produced visuals to account for the organizations and simultaneous movements in the squares, and interpreted the readable effects. From the observation of photos and film sequences, the paths and variations were analyzed and translated graphically, without the use of software. The drawings are made from a zoom of 150 meters of perimeter for 3 minutes.

Each intersection diagram aims to give identifiable points for all the movements and characterize each culture of crossing.

At the end of this part, 4 guests-accomplices react to this survey from their respective disciplines and with their respective perceptions.

The path of the movements is registered in space. JL Design and Korb, CCTV Documentary idents, www.edition Kord.tv, in Felton, Nicholas, 2016, Photoviz, Gestalten edition.

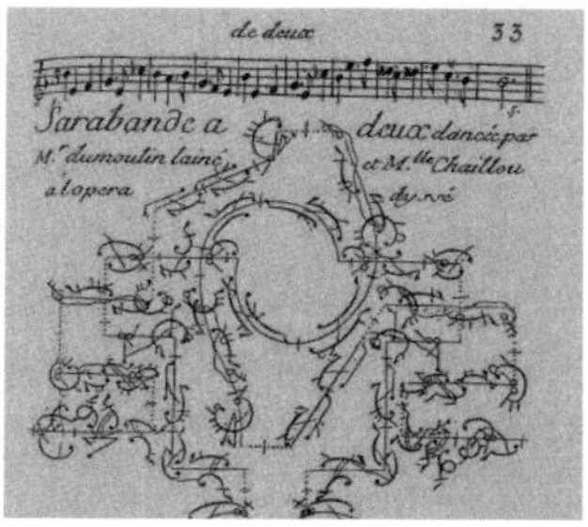

The first representations of simultaneous movements and their traces, from the Feuillet notation (circa 1700) of a Sarabande, a dance for two people, published in "La belle dance", 1995, Vand Dieren éditeur.

Sharing space between modes of transport

A tailor-made cocktail

The graphs deal with multi-modality. The modal split is derived from a visual count on the video footage and cross-checked with city data. If all the intersections are very busy, the modal distribution changes a lot depending on the country. The number of mobile elements during 3 minutes on each square varies from 240 to 730.

Each culture and each place gives a different distribution of modes. This shows that each situation requires a unique solution. With different travel mode distribution and mobile maneuvering, the crossing organizations cannot be similar. The flexibility of pedestrians[22] and small vehicles makes it possible to divide the crossing surfaces and limit the protective equipment that pushes people to speed and impose their passage. The Japanese intersection is the busiest with a majority of pedestrians which allows a high density and maximum flexibility of movement. The modal share is the opposite in China, with a majority of cars. In terms of atmosphere, comfort is greater in Tokyo and Copenhagen. This is not directly related to the number of mobile elements, but rather to the adaptation of the crossing system to the quantity and local distribution of them. The maximum modal diversity in Old Delhi or Hanoi loses in safety but gains a lot in terms of diversity with self-regulating keys and a certain dynamism. The urban spectacle is present in many crossings. This sharing of space and time is a key factor of the atmosphere.

However, there is a limiting factor with the quantity of mobile elements on a single site. Saturation can be avoided with modal transfers and the use of smaller vehicules allowing more agile movements and adapted and reactive management, as in London. But beyond a certain quantity the space is saturated, it is no longer possible to move and above all it becomes anxious atmosphere because all freedom of movement is once again constrained, without any of the escape routes explored above.

Finally, the evolution of the intersections studied shows that during the last two years new kinds of modal sharing has been made possible, notably for bicycles in London and Beijing.

The tailor-made cocktail is in the diversification of the modes and a possible restraint in the quantities, according to the capacities of the sites. This cocktail sets the mood.

22 Pedestrian flexibility in relation to the car: "Pedestrians can twist, duck, bend, turn sharply, and therefore, unlike motorists, can safely count on being able to extricate themselves in the last few milliseconds before impending impact." Goffman, Erving, 1971, Relations in Public: Microstudies of the Public Order, New York, Routledge.

Old Delhi, India

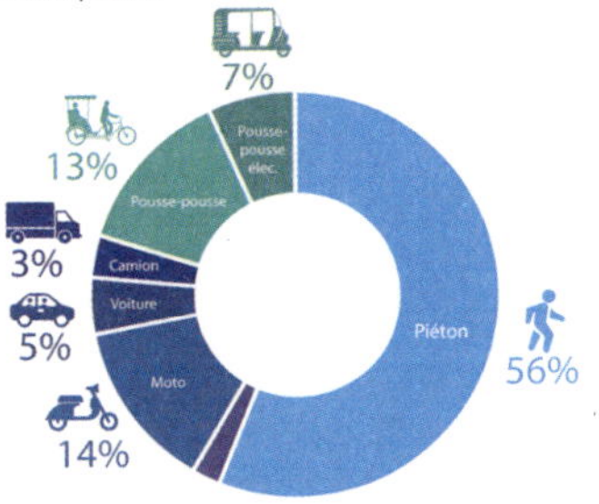

Copenhagen / Denmark

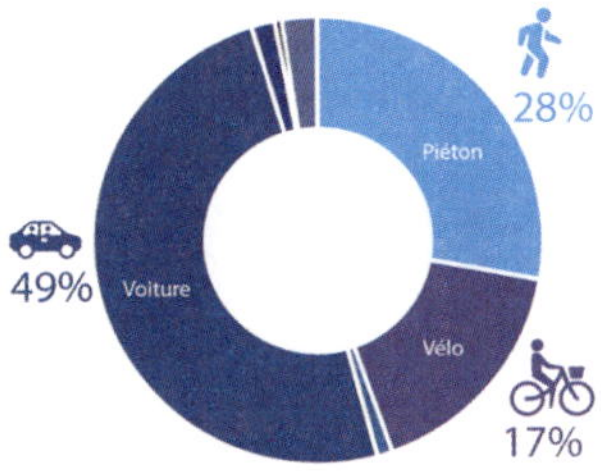

Tokyo / Japan

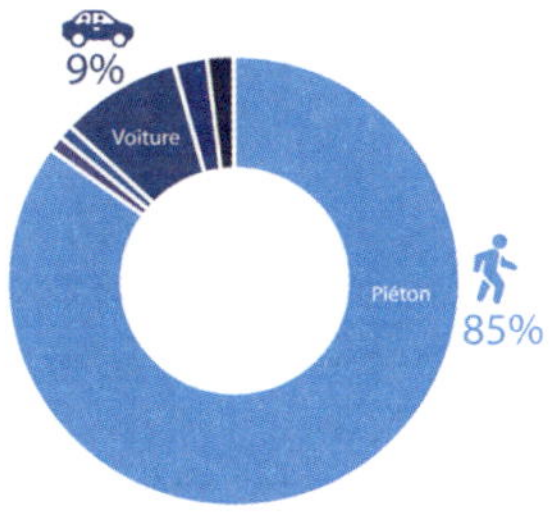

Hanoi / Vietnam

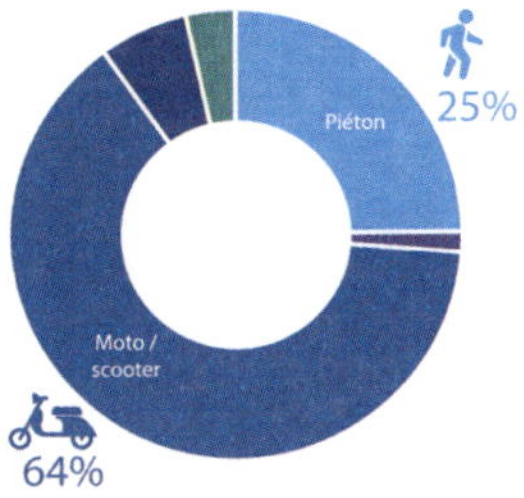

London / England

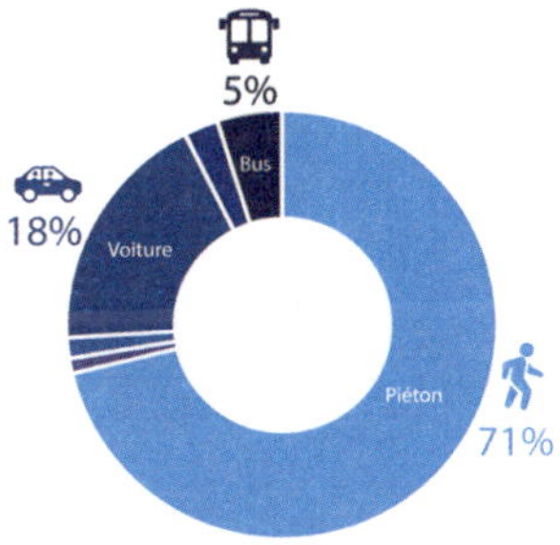

Lagos, Nigeria

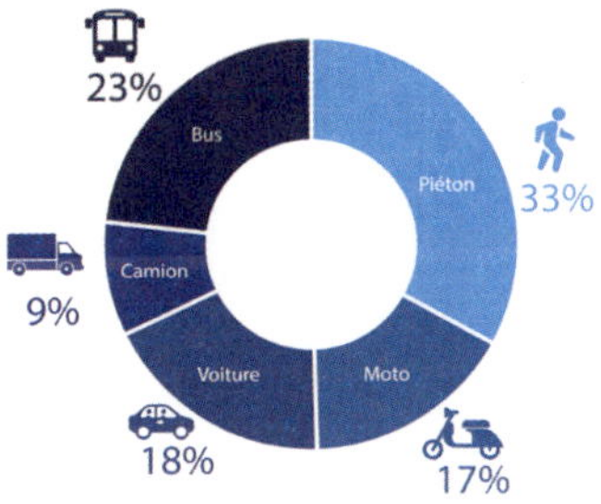

Sao Paulo / Brazil

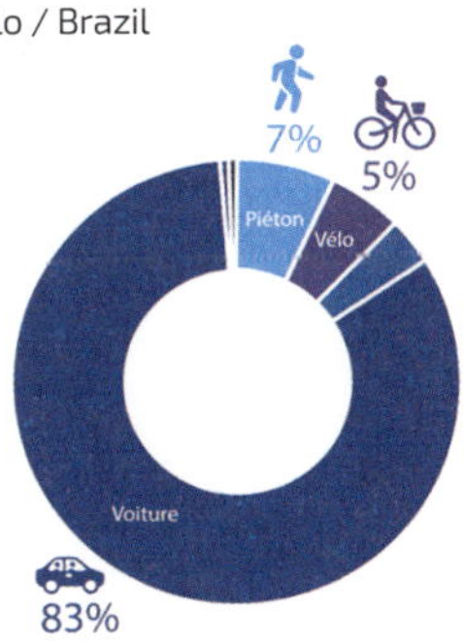

Beijing / China

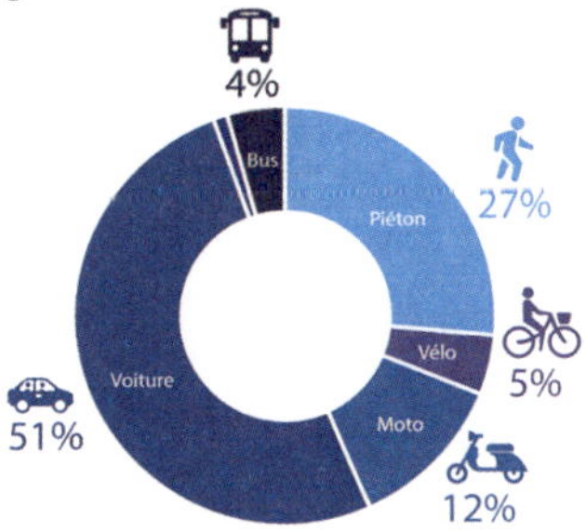

Sharing: The distribution of the modes of travel within the 8 sites

Thermal flow of simultaneous movements

Accept slow speeds

The illustrations show the speed at which all the mobile elements cross the intersection over 3 minutes. This synthesis gives a color for each level of speed: the colors go from the coldest (blue) for slow, to the warmest (yellow) for fast. The speed variations are also indicated, as well as the nature of the paths: straight for vehicles and winding for pedestrians.

In order to get away from the dependence on the "fastest", it is interesting to observe that, contrary to the increase in speed for long distances, with the high-speed train and the airplane, speeds within cities are decreasing.[23] Saturation and modal diversification are the first explanations. The increase in the role of pedestrians is another. At intersections, the slowdown is obvious for the crossing, but we also observe a very different sharing of space between sites: a lot of space for pedestrians in London, a lot for cars in Sao Paulo. The illustrations show crossings with a majority of slow speeds in Lagos or Hanoi, and others with fast speeds in Sao Paulo, Beijing or Copenhagen. The blue and purple shades tend to represent small mobile elements, while the green and yellow shades represent mostly motor vehicles.

Even though the number of accidents is an important indicator in the study of intersections, we prefer to look at the causes and therefore above all the attitudes of the mobile elements. We thus note a very different position with regard to compliance with the codes: very strong in Denmark and Japan (thick line for motor vehicles) and a more reactive and diffuse attitude in China for example. The differences in speed and rhythm often create accident points. To limit them, in Old Delhi, it is observed that slow movements generally mark micro-stops, allowing one to adjust one's trajectory and to brush against the crossing mobile element. This type of crossing is clearly avoided in the case of a traffic light intersection, with the mobile elements being kept at a distance thanks to time. The difference in size of the vehicles is policed by the traffic lights. In Hanoi, the varying speed capabilities of the mobile elements could cause an imbalance. This seems to be compensated by a relatively homogeneous, slow and continuous general movement, in order to manage crossing between mobile elements.

For pedestrians, several speeds are sometimes observed, as in London: those in a hurry, who cross in two stages outside the time reserved for pedestrians, and those who are slower, who respect the rules. Some slow paths sometimes cross fast-moving areas by taking advantage of very short gaps: temporal, in the flow of traffic, and spatial, between the traffic lanes. Thus, within a strict management of crossings, different attitudes related to speed and patience of users are taken into account.

Finally, the case of China shows vehicles stuck in the middle of the intersection, having to slow down to negotiate the exit. This intersection therefore mixes moderate and fast speeds.

Agreeing to slow down makes it easier to cross the road. Thus, the more moderate the speed, the more possible it is to cross.

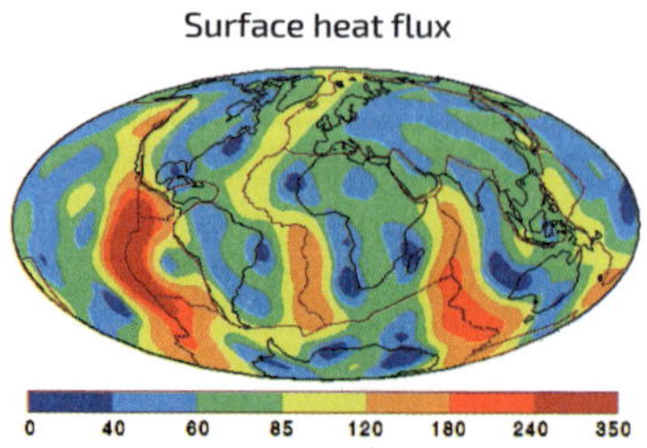

Global heat flow map (spherical harmonic, degree 12), 2001, Global heat flow data, Geological Sciences, Univ. of Michigan.

23 In Paris intra-muros, the average speed has dropped from 16.6 km/h in 2002, to 12.3 km/h in 2018, source: Le bulletin de l'observatoire des déplacements à Paris, 2019, Marie de Paris /DVD.

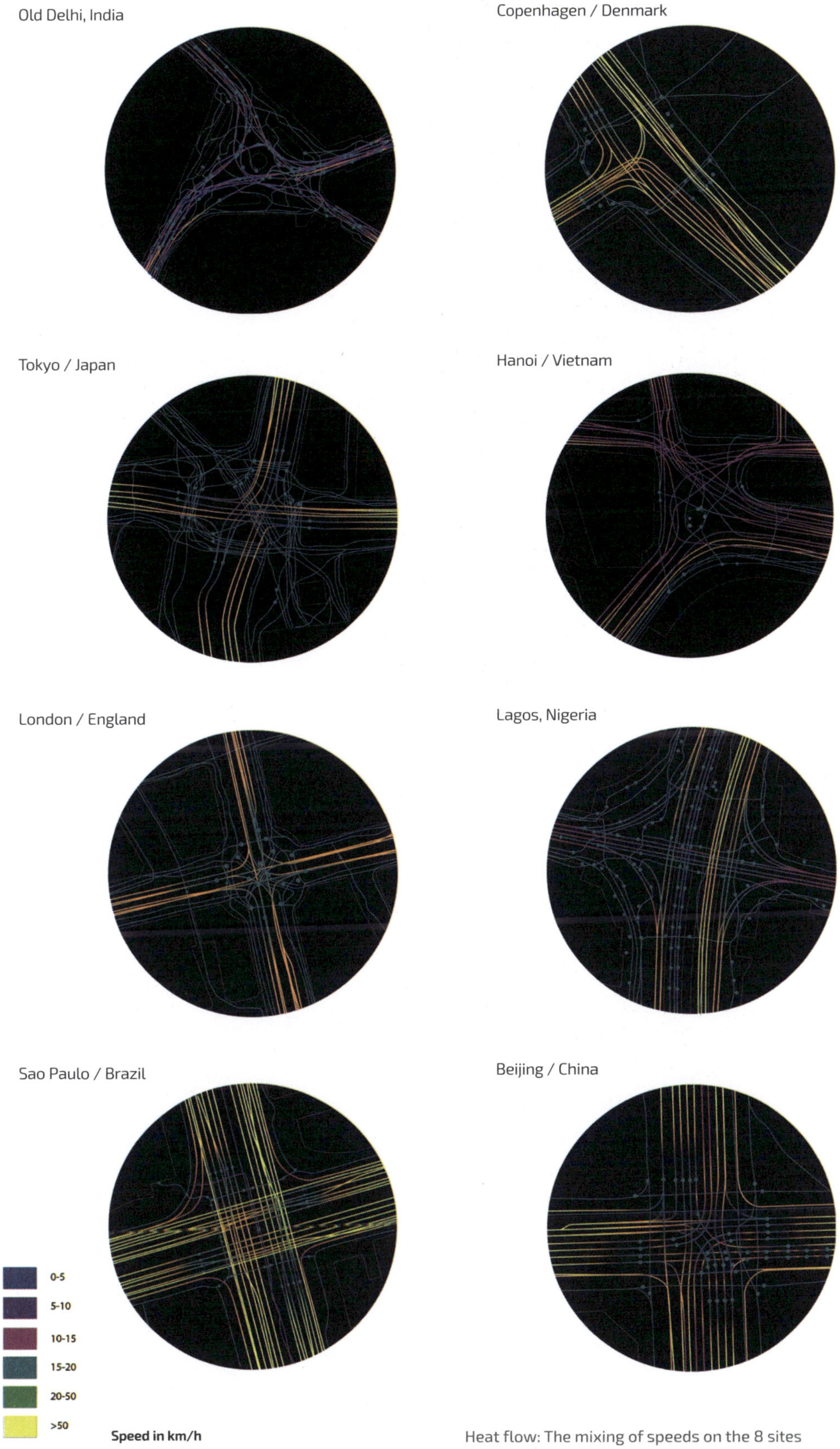

Heat flow: The mixing of speeds on the 8 sites

Old Delhi, India

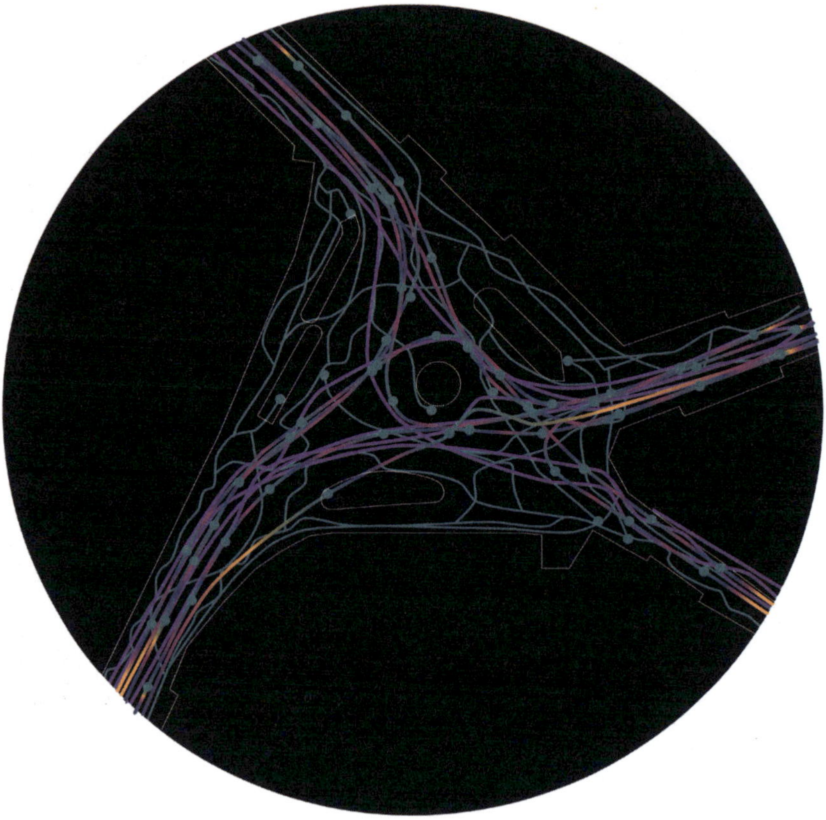

London, England

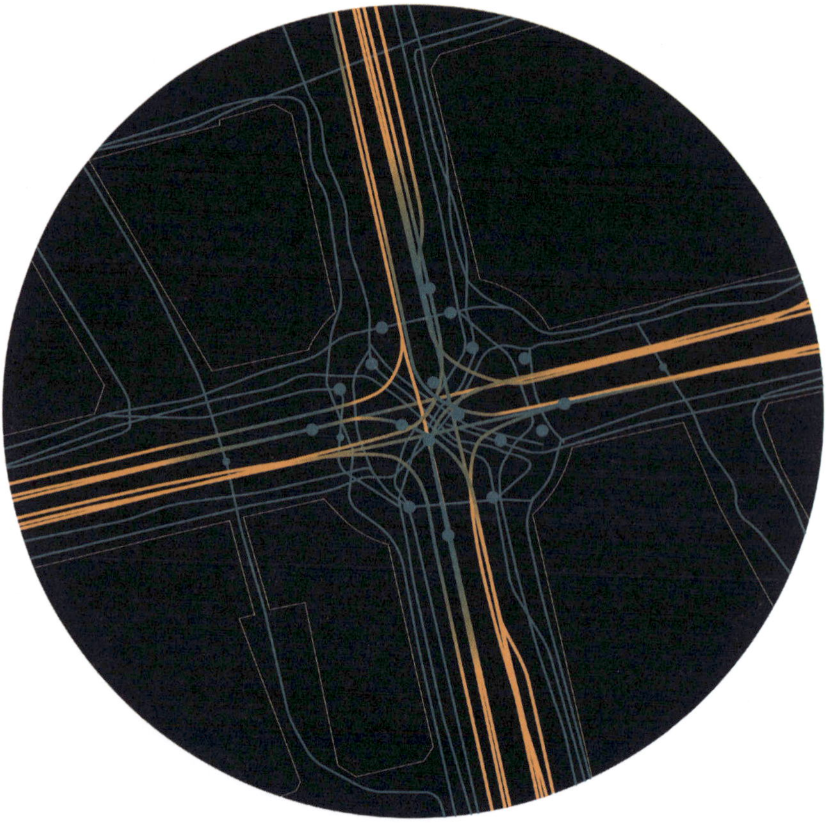

Lagos, Nigeria

Beijing, China

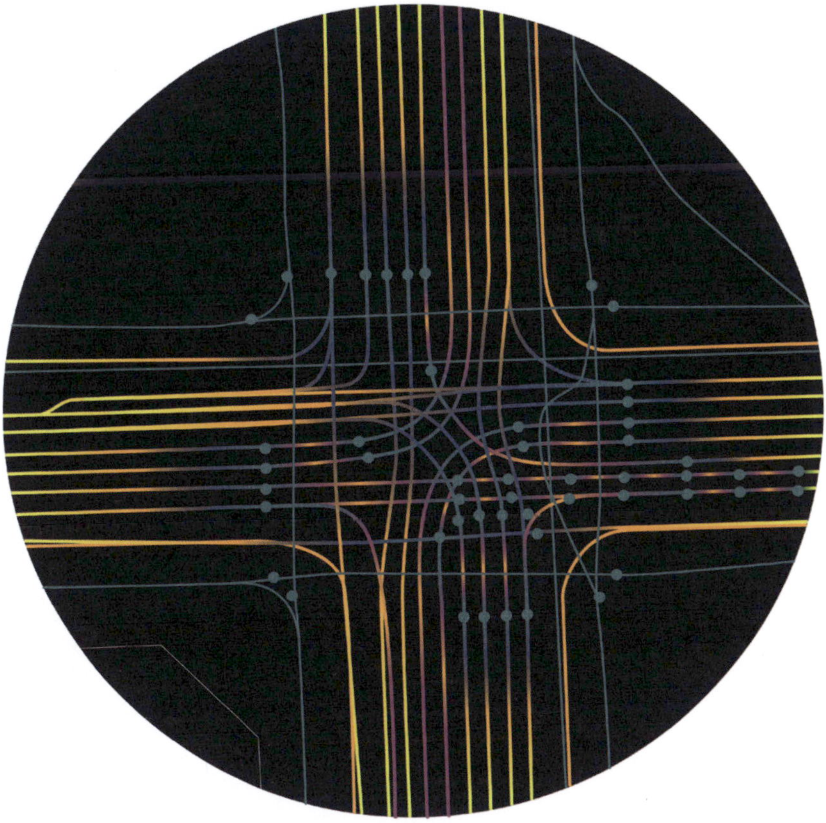

Musical score of stops on the trajectories

From macro crossroads to micro crossings

Making diagrams of the intersections shows the paths of the mobile elements and the stopped moments for 3 minutes. A short time is represented by a small point, a long time by a large point, whatever the nature of the mobile elements. This makes it possible to distinguish the stops in the movements and the fluidity of the trajectory.

The complexity of the operations provides leads for improvement in situations of saturation and blockage that can be disentangled according to different organizations of time and priorities, across cultures. Movements in Old Delhi encourage different motorized and non-motorized modes. Co-presence is managed with jerky movements, with micro-stops. Hanoi accommodates different modes in the same way, but the movement is much slower and continuous. Mixing is possible. The movement in Lagos has long interruptions as minibuses crowd the street waiting for passengers, and the highways are generally heavily congested. China has a similar case of saturation due to an abundance of vehicles.

While movements in Brazil, England, Japan and Denmark are restricted, we find more impositions on "left-turns" in Denmark and Brazil, making them faster than the other two, but more restrictive to freedom of movement. This results in a need to manage speed, but also with the ability to stop, slow down and brake, in the case of a large number of crossings and travel modes.

For traffic light intersections, the trajectories are simpler, with straight lines and often 90° turns. These movements are possible for all vehicles, including trucks and public transport. Certain options are excluded with vehicles that are too large, as they are dangerous, while flexibility is possible with small vehicles. The heavy presence of vehicles at certain sites excludes porous crossings. Short distances and small vehicles, such as mopeds or scooters, are factors that facilitate micro-crossings and thus greater freedom of movement, in co-existence with other vehicles.

The frequency and duration of stops on each of the routes give very different impressions at different sites:

- in Hanoi, the atmosphere is fluid, despite the very slow speed,
- in Lagos, the atmosphere is tense and uncertain,
- in Sao Paulo and Copenhagen, the musical scores appear a little strict.

These atmospheres are more or less spread out over the sites, with a concentration of stops at the crossing points in London, or a complete spread over the intersection in Lagos.

Excerpt from the score of Ravel's Boléro

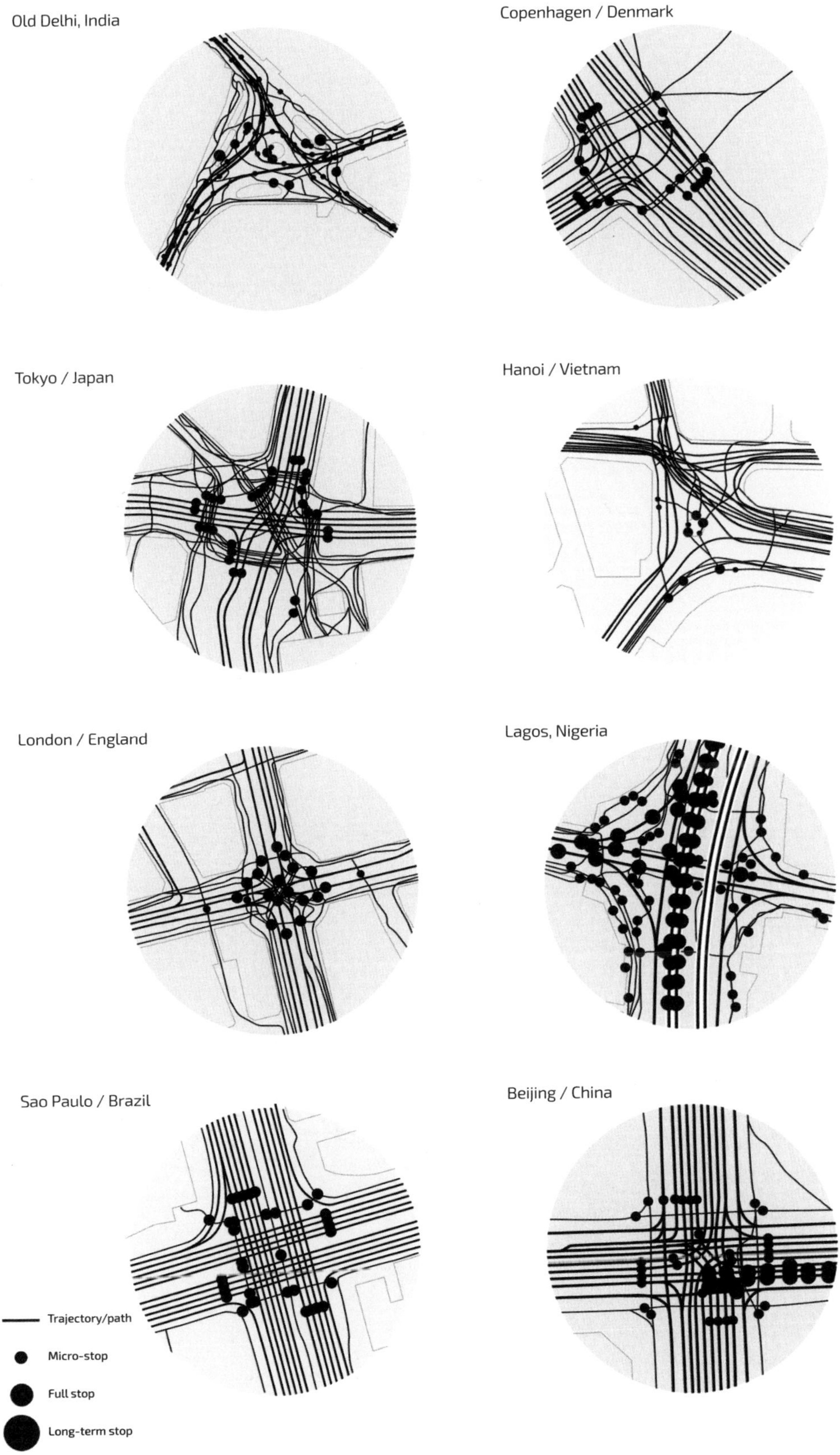

Musical score: The paths and stops of the 8 sites

Old Delhi, India

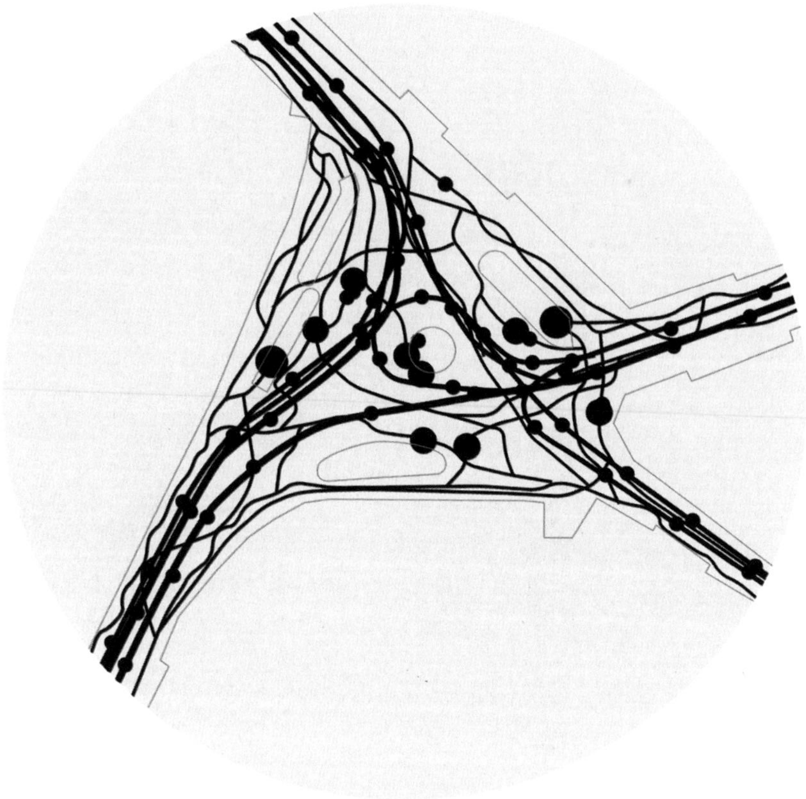

London, England

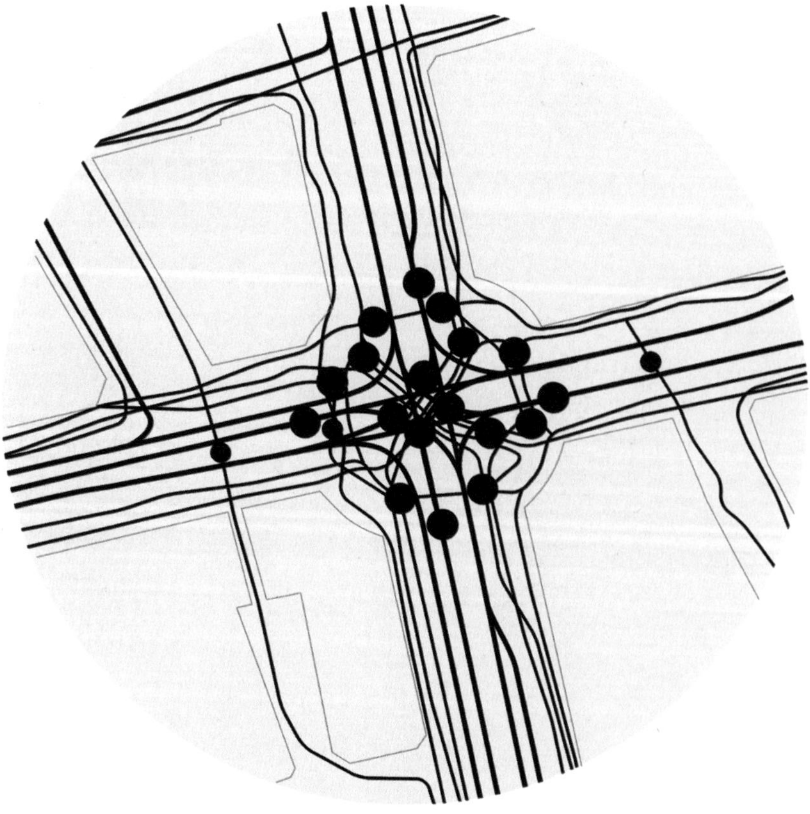

Lagos, Nigeria

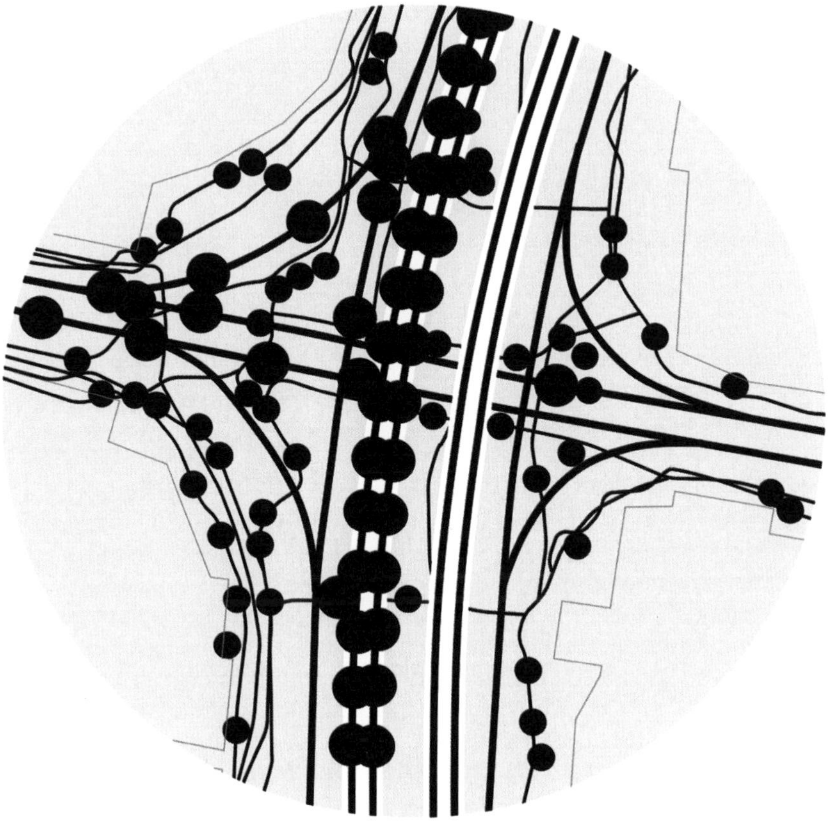

Beijing, China

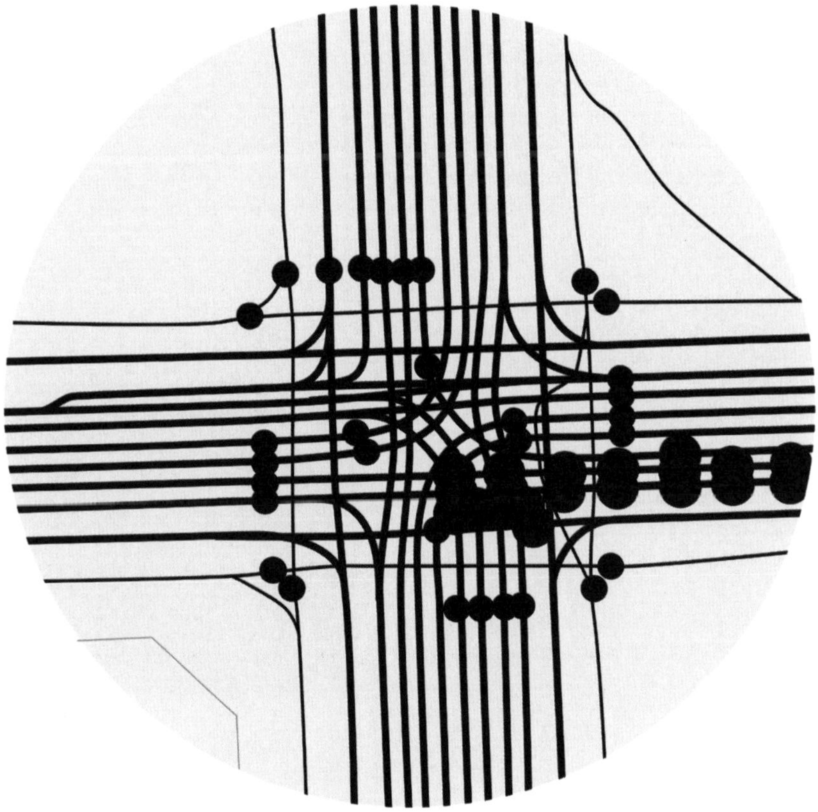

Chrono-drawing on the variations of movement
The possibility and ability to improvise

Making diagrams of intersections is difficult without activity to show movement, but too much movement in one image makes it difficult to synthesize analytically. The diagrams below, inspired by Eadweard Muybridge's superimposed photographic images, represent points that are narrowed for slowing down and spaced out for accelerating. This chrono-illustration allows to read simultaneously the visible or felt movement on the intersection, over a time of 3 minutes. All the trajectories are represented to illustrate all the simultaneous movements specific to the site.

The drawn representation of the movements of the square, without its constructed framework, makes it possible to read a kind of global graphic signature formed by the ephemeral trajectories. A highly contrasted pattern for each square becomes legible. The regular and precise movements of Sao Paulo or Copenhagen are distinguished from the abundant and sinuous movements of Hanoi or even London. The possibility of moving more freely comes from the maneuverability of the mobile element and the attitude of the user. We bring it closer to the reactive attitude of surfers who advance on a moving ground, but also the acceptance, even the appreciation, of being on a ground in perpetual movement. This ability to improvise is necessary to move in the city. Reactivity can also be allowed and encouraged.

The graphs also show the radical nature of traffic light intersections and flow separation, which spread movements over large areas.

The changing context of an intersection requires a dynamic vision of the space. The complexity of the changes requires tactics in relation to recurring movements. These representations give a reading of the variations and make it possible to anticipate, to be ready, to integrate the changes that are recurrent. This also makes it possible to envisage adaptations between modes, as the co-presence of a tramway and pedestrians has long since shown. Taking into account the other mobile element is very obvious in Hanoi, with paths in interaction contrary to the regular functioning of traffic light intersections, like in Sao Paulo.

The resulting pattern of movements appears to be less related to spatial geometry than to the managing of crossings by the mobile elements.

These representations of chrono-design and partitioning give information on the negotiations between the paths with the indication of stopping points at the moment of crossing. The red traffic light time of more than a minute is reduced to less than a second in intersections in Hanoi or Delhi, for a movement decision. This movement control is tied to the experience of little time and the unexpected, and to the users' ability to react. As such, individual perceptions have repercussions on the organization of the whole crossing system. The waiting phases that are necessary (or not) in passage decisions appear highly variable depending on the contexts.

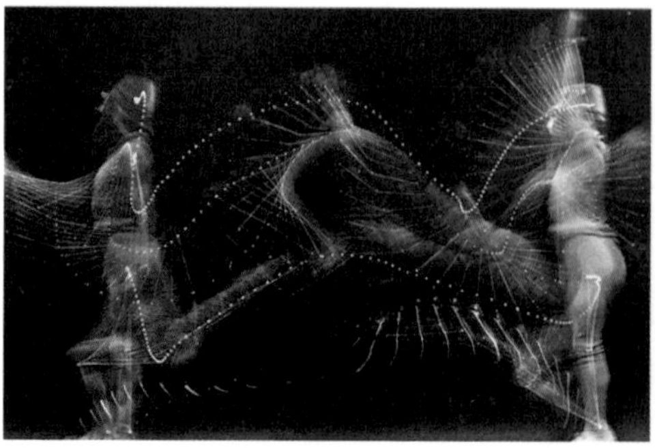

Chrono-photography of Demeny G., 1906, Long jump without momentum © INSEP.

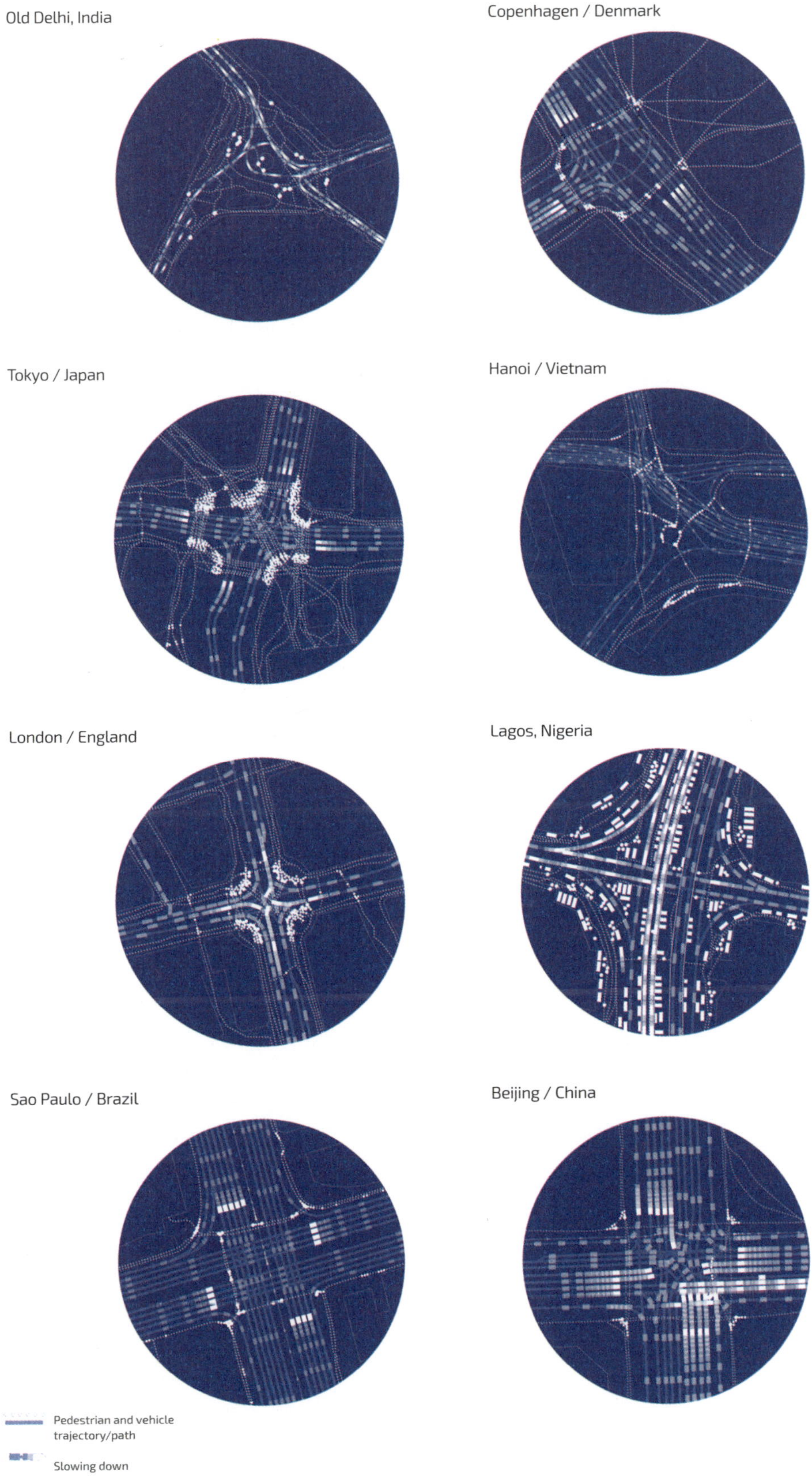

Chrono-drawing: The variations of movements, slowdowns and accelerations on the 8 sites

Tokyo, Japan

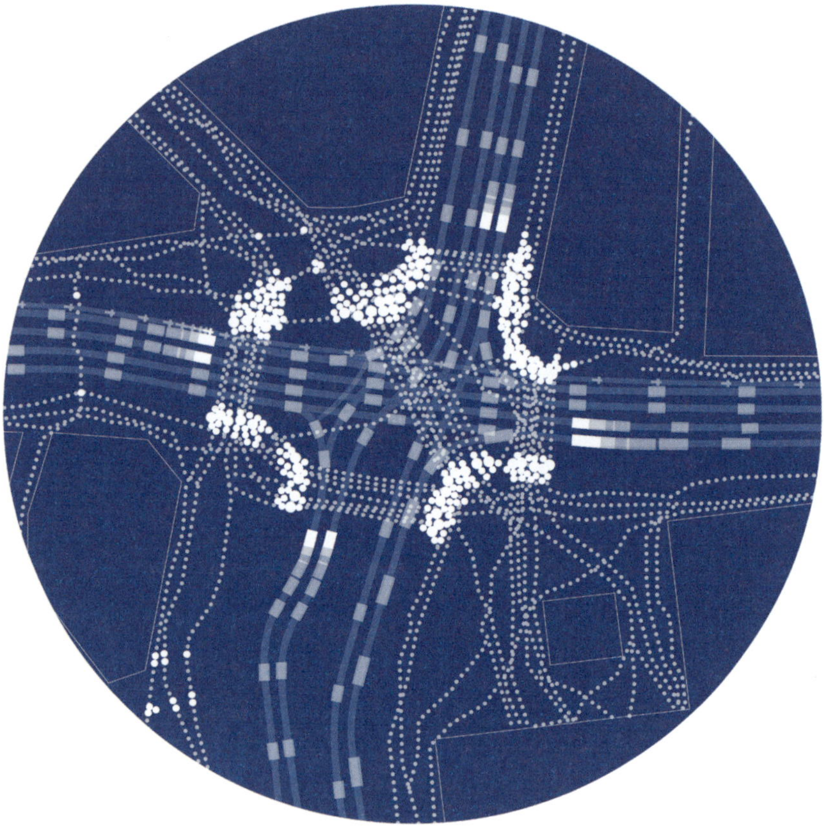

Sao Paulo, Brazil

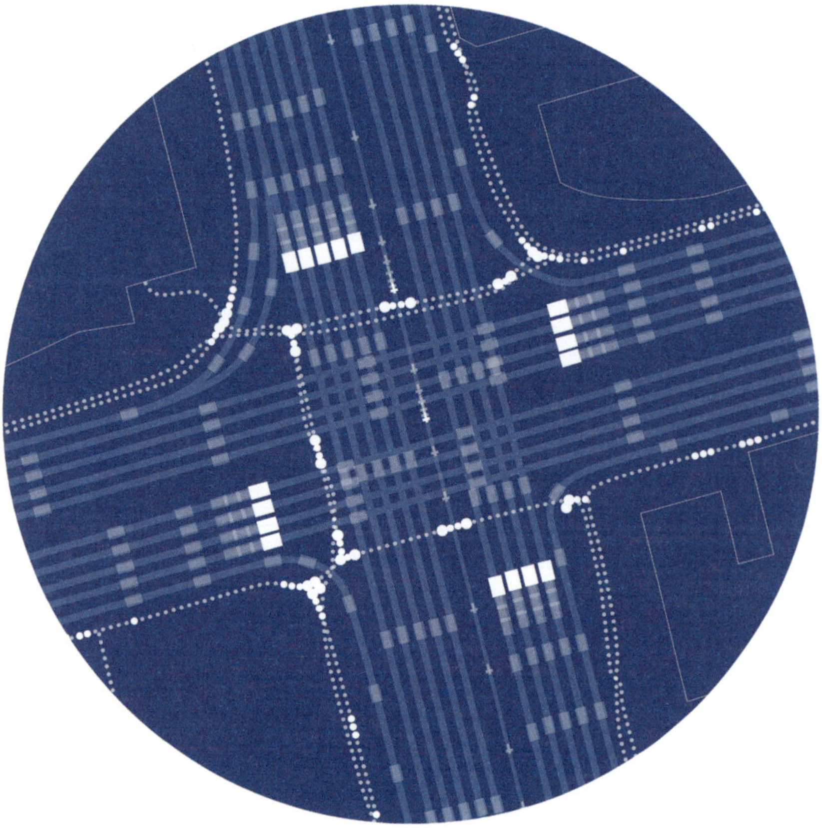

Copenhaguen, Denmark

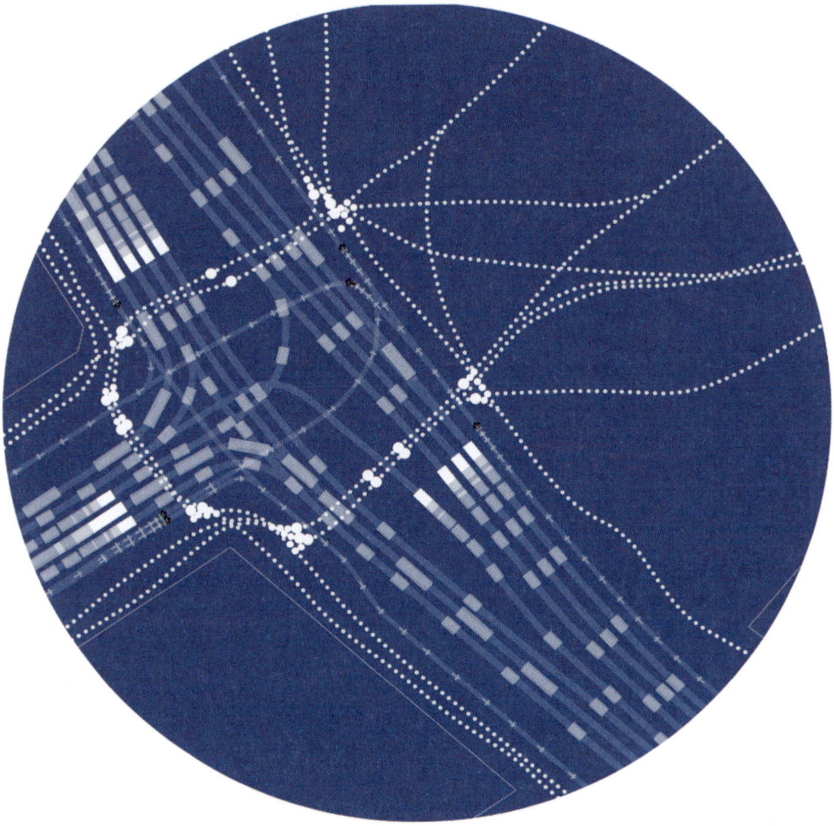

Hanoi, Vietnam

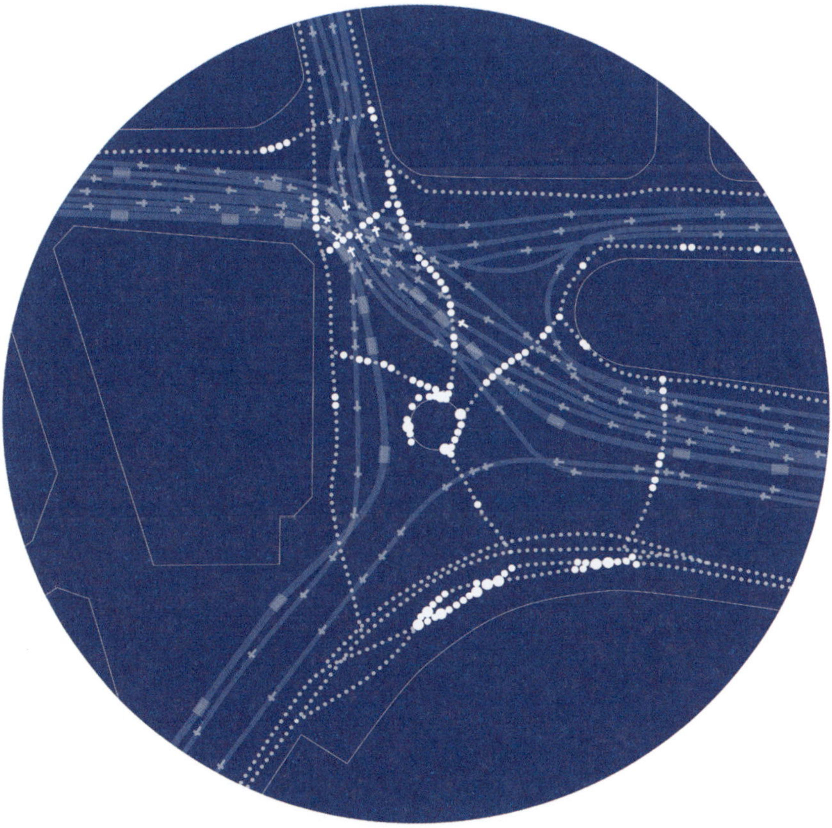

Weather forecast of intense and mild crossings
Use the dance floor and oases

The diagrams show the crossing spaces between mobile ele ments of similar speeds (in green) slow and safe, and diffe rent speeds (in blue), intense and turbulent. This reveals where empty, the spaces without crossing.

The division of the public space by the trajectories shows a very strong and straight fragmentation on the intersections with traffic lights and a much more organic one on the intersections with small roundabouts and significant room for pedestrians. An architecture of crossings is drawn with a radical and geometric imprint or random and curved ones. Faced with the large empty space of the square, a distribution of spaces according to the movements is made. Invisible to the user, this structuring of the space appears on the representations opposite.

This eventual organization surely influences the behavior of mobile people, whether they are in vehicles or not. Some slow and intense zones are indicated.

The intensity of the superposition of the trajectories shows strongly solicited and fast spaces, where the passage will be difficult. On the contrary, in other places, the few crossings show quieter areas, where stopping and pausing would be possible. Thus, the square can be broken down into "oasis" spaces, calm and for relaxation, set back from the crossings, and "dance floor" spaces, animated and requiring reactivity, to move and cross. In an oasis space, ease dominates. On the dance floor, it is necessary to be alert and to get going.

This partition can be extended to a distinction between multi-modal and single-modal spaces, with those that can change and those that are fixed. The separation of spaces for pedestrians and vehicles is one solution, but so is the temporal sequencing with a time given to pedestrians by traffic lights. In all cases, the possibility of having stable and simple spaces (for local cultures) appears necessary to allow local uses and not only passage. The contraction of movements and presence in public space allows a composition of passing and exchange activity.

The diversity of the types and areas of crossings results in squares that are pacified, thanks to cultural codes, or very intense, with traffic lights.

The public space is in strong tension according to the place given to crossings with varying speeds.

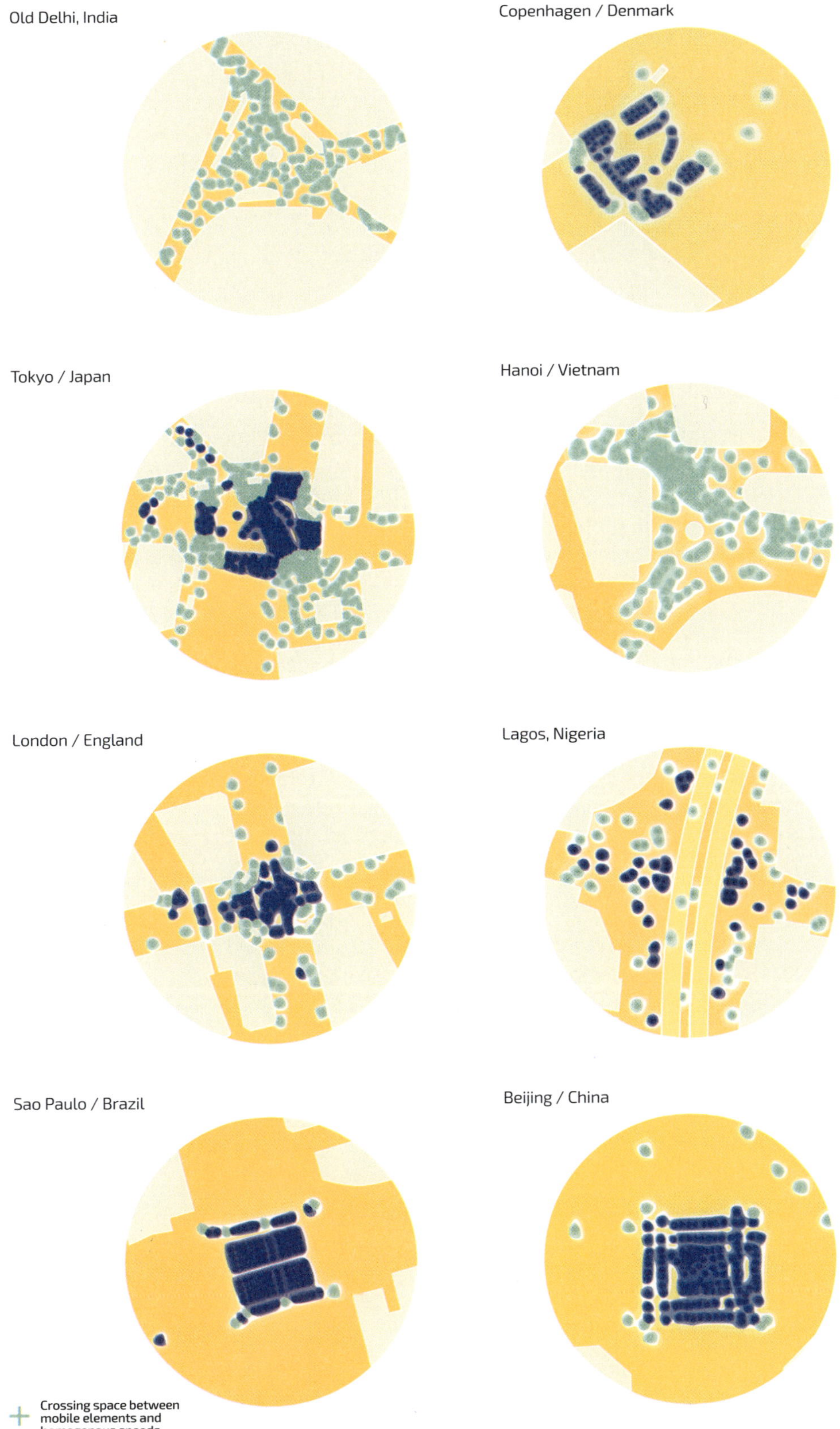

Crossing Weather: Awakening spaces with crossings and relaxation of the 8 sites

Tokyo, Japan

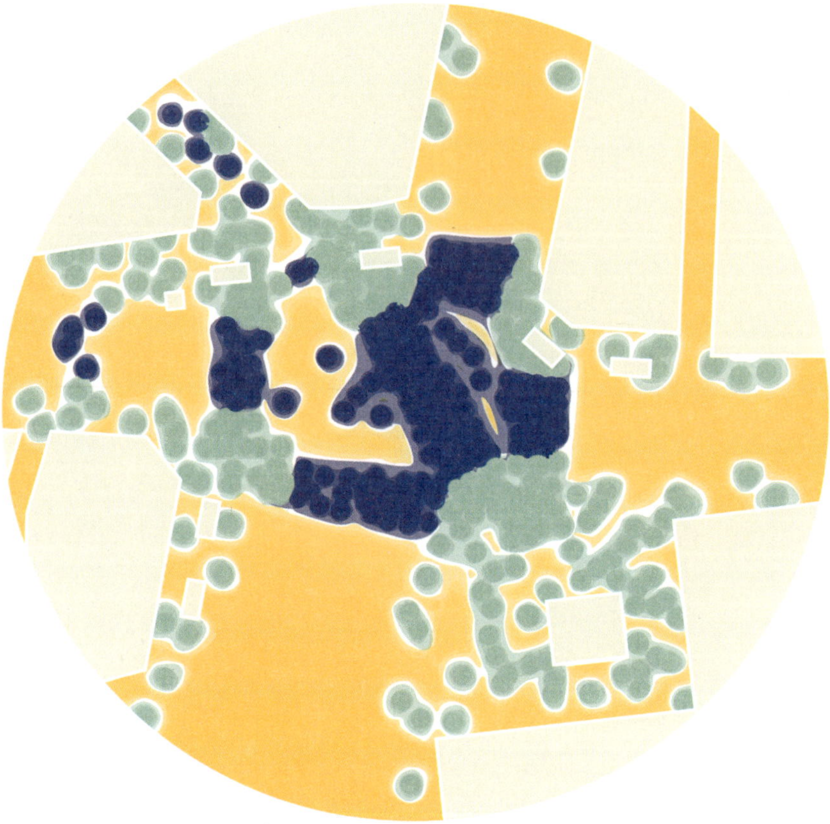

Sao Paulo, Brazil

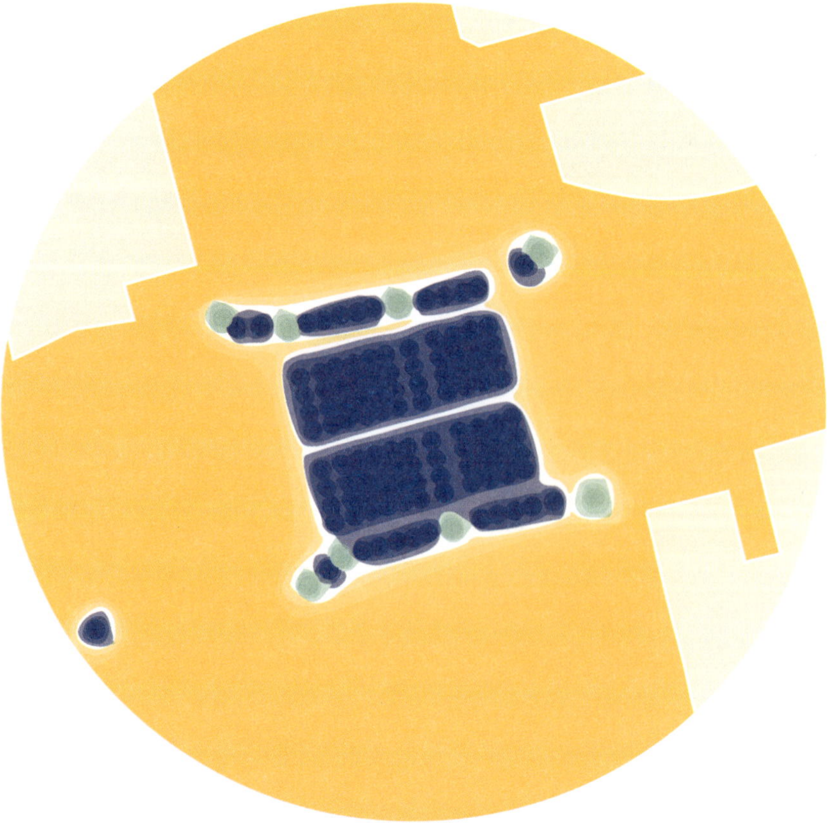

Copenhaguen, Denmark

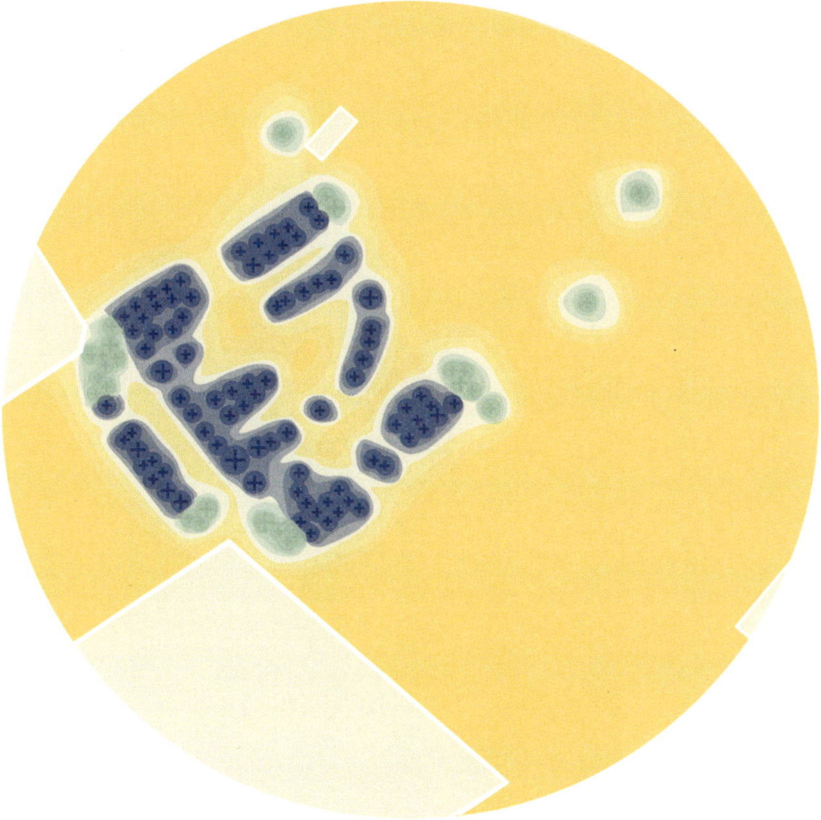

Hanoi, Vietnam

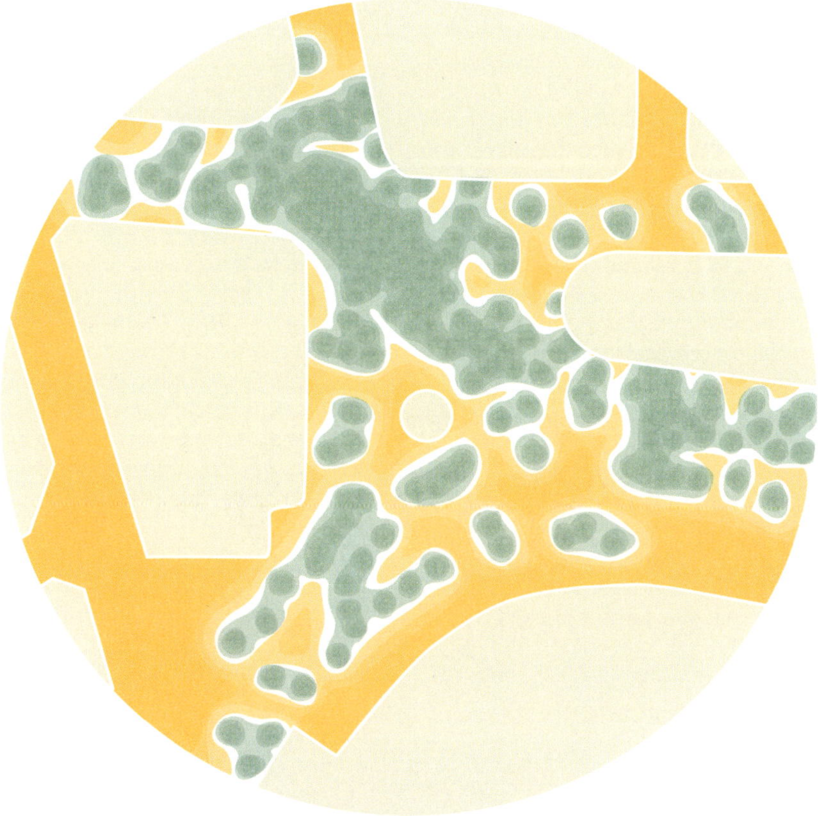

Eric Alonzo
Architect and historian

Professor, ocs/ausser (CNRS umr 3329)
School of Architecture of the City and Territories of Paris-Est
Gustave Eiffel University

How do architects deal with flows?

The arrival of mechanized vehicles – automobiles and motorized two-wheelers – at the beginning of the 20th century disrupted the rhythms and geometries of urban flows, which until then had been dominated by animal locomotion (pedestrians, horse riders, pack animals, horse-drawn carriages, etc.). At first glance, we could therefore place at this time the birth of the urbanistic concerns to which this survey bears. However, this type of work is part of a tradition that predates the appearance of automobile traffic.

Already in the 18th century, the projects for squares under Louis XIV sought to dissolve the congestion of cars in the major urban intersections, by widening the crossing points and creating new branches. Although the organization of traffic flows became a major issue at this time, it was not the subject of specific studies. For that, we have to wait for the Catalan engineer Ildefons Cerdà who, in his 1863 diagrams, points out with arrows the different trajectories that cross a four-branch intersection: not only those of cars, but also those of horse riders, "single" pedestrians and "loaded" pedestrians. This analysis led him to propose that the flows could be untangled by a system of refuge islands placed in the center of vast crossroads. In 1906, the Parisian architect Eugène Hénard expanded on these graphic analyses of urban traffic at intersections, focusing more exclusively on the traffic of cars - which were still mostly horse-drawn - and led to the invention of the roundabout system: a one-way street designed to avoid accidents by converting intersecting trajectories into tangent trajectories

In the meantime, the Viennese architect Camillo Sitte, who was very hostile to the hegemony of technicist approaches to public space, also depicted the trajectory of cars at intersections in The Art of Building Cities (1889), in order to legitimize his artistic proposals. But the originality of his contribution probably lies in the observation of snow-covered squares on which the flow of cars is printed. This materialization of movement allows us to see, between the "channels of communication", the existence of "dead spots of traffic" which would determine the implantation of monumental aediculae. It is thus through an empirical process, based on the analysis of the shape of existing square-intersections – and the geometry of the flows they generate – that Sitte draws up "rules" intended to be applied to future developments.

Placed in this long disciplinary lineage, this essay gives an account of an urban space that has become much more complex, governed by numerous rules, norms and regulatory systems – notably traffic lights. But the most fundamental difference with the work of the "founders" of urbanism probably lies in the place given to the temporalities of movement as well as in the anthropological approach sensitive to the cultural variations that come into play in the forms and rhythms of the flows observed in these different cities of the world.

Fabrice Guillot
Choreographer

Director and founder of the vertical dance company Retouramont, France and World.
Former rock-climbing route opener

Matter is motion that densifies

"Matter is motion that densifies", was first said by theorists of the Big Bang. It refers to the mountain range emerging from the earth's crust by telluric thrusts that has come to be in our landscape.

The form of the urban material with its flows is constructed totally differently from one city to another, from one continent to another. Architecture reveals the ways in which people relate to one another in each society. The buildings, beyond their functionality, are the concretization of an aesthetic, of natural materials at hand, of concepts of living together.

The intersection is the space where trajectories meet, it is the place of a relationship that this time remains in motion. One might think that homogeneous signage on all continents would produce the same effects on flows. In reality, intersections of the entire world are places of choreographies as diverse as there are modes of human interaction.

What proximity do we accept between bodies? What room do we leave for improvisation in the intersections of our trajectories? How do we organize the tacit rules of right-of-way that reveal the place left to the other? This survey outlines some answers.

The intersections of the world as objects of study are as fascinating for the choreographer that I am as they are for the urbanist of movement that Stéphane Lemoine is.

My experience of the Place de l'Étoile in Paris is similar to a feeling of improvisation in dance, trying not to go towards contact dance. The minimal distance between the objects allows the movement, the accidental contact stops the flow.

An intersection usually regulated by traffic lights sometimes becomes wild again during a break. The flashing orange lights connect us to each user of the place we cross, we must understand the project of the other, even perceive his/her character. Another sense is developed which is called in dance "listening", I am aware of the place of the other and his/her trajectory, I move in my turn by integrating his /her presence and his/her behavior. I am obliged to understand the other in order to continue my trajectory, our collective presence draws a global choreography.

My very perception of space is sharpened, I move from my somnambulistic line to a broader understanding of the site, its dimensions, and its structure. I make my choices of stops, bypasses, acceleration... I am no longer an element of a managed flow, but an actor with all those who share the hidden site.

The hidden signage changes the space crossed, we go from an intersection with anonymous and automated flows to a place of relationship that requires sharpening our senses while leaving to each one a part of improvisation, of creativity. It is this interaction between the users/inhabitants of the shared space that characterizes a square.

Thanks to this relationship, perhaps we can once again take ownership of these crossing spaces, imagine their future, transform them.

Our intertwined journeys then transform the matter.

Philippe Massé
Flow engineer

President and founder of Eco-mobilities Territories and Connections, France

Milestones through urban crossings

Speeds and saturation
The flow of traffic on a city road outside the intersection is about 1,800 vehicles per hour, i.e., 1 every 2 seconds.

This flow rate, considered as a "maximum average" in the technical literature, is then weighted by factors, some of which are related to urban life: intersections, pedestrian crossings, parking and delivery maneuvers. These disruptive factors are pushed to the extreme at the Indian intersection. In Europe, the maximum flow is reached in the city at a speed of about 40 km/h. Beyond that, the flow decreases. Thus, the traffic efficiency of an urban development is not linked to high speeds.

Motivated by the safety of users, we have gone from 60 to 50 km/h in France, then increasingly to 30 or even 20 km/h in certain more residential areas.
The saturation of cities also plays a role: beyond a certain flow rate, speed decreases. It would therefore be in the interest of all to adopt fairly low speeds for motorized methods, which would reduce the differences between the various modes without greatly increasing travel times. Travel time in cities is essentially affected by lane congestion.

Mode combinations
Moreover, the diversity of modes poses a problem of division of space and, in some cases, of time.

When we plan a square or an intersection, we realize that it is difficult to organize the operation of crossings in compliance with the various standards (regulatory times for pedestrians, bicycles, cars, lane widths). This is quite clear for a space crossed by a tramway which has different kinematic characteristics from the other modes, no flexibility in its trajectories and which, moreover, must maintain an attractive commercial speed, with most often a priority at the traffic lights of the intersections. In the technical model, we reach a limit in terms of space and time division.

The example of the Chinese intersection shows that the technical organization, despite the considerable right-of-way, also has its limits, particularly in regard to the right-of-way of the crossing.

In some cases, it is possible to allow a few specific modes to coexist, as in Copenhagen or in Paris on rue François Miron. However, in France, cars are difficult to integrate into this sharing.

The division of time into distinct phases, ordered in traffic light cycles, devoted to one mode or group of modes can sometimes lead to relatively long waiting times. This waiting time is felt to be too long, as it forces people to stand still. In Europe, it is generally considered that a cycle time of 2 minutes is a limit that should not be exceeded.

Agility
Otherwise, we observe that the more agile a mode is, the more likely it is to disregard the indications given by the signals and to cross. For pedestrians, the most reactive mode, crossing the lanes is done as quickly as possible, as seen in the London intersection.

This agility also leads to behavior that is difficult to reconcile with organized flows, divided into sequences. In fact, it is the "potential speed" of each mode that leads to a supposed superiority of the fastest users. This can be seen quite clearly with personal modes of transport, some two-wheelers and even cycles.

Careful organization
The technique, essential for the development of projects must therefore serve everyone and not be content to allow all "users" to pass as scientifically as possible. We should not hesitate, for example, to create real pedestrian phases in certain traffic light intersections, as in Japan. We can also resort to small urban roundabouts whose main qualities are to reduce vehicle speeds and, ultimately, to be more readable than a complex traffic light intersection for all users. No one can give in to automatic operation, whether as users or as managers. In any case it will be necessary to take the data from the start, to spend time on the ground, to make an urban project, and to work without prejudice.

It seems to me that we should aim to homogenize and reduce speeds, limit the division of space into strips and adjust waiting times for everyone.

Stéphane Juguet
Urban anthropologist

Urban anthropologist
Director of the imaginary factory
What Time Is I.T. France.
Graduate of the doctoral school
of the University of Technology of
Compiègne (UTC)

The "Quatre-Chemins" (4 paths) intersection, a rite ... of transgressive passage

Intersections are not an insignificant technical object. It is a cultural marker and an indicator of urban practices that vary according to the continents but also the districts. To be convinced of this, let's go to the gates of Paris, to Pantin, to the cosmopolitan intersection of the 4 paths.

"Here, it's a mess!!" we are told. Indeed, the urban agitation is intense, not to say chaotic. We come across pedestrians and cyclists who weave in and out of the cars, following only one rule: uncontrolled crossing. On the sidewalks, the activity is just as "messy". At the traffic lights, a young Roma man pulls up to the line of cars stuck in traffic, offering cold drinks. The congestion becomes a godsend for his "trafficking". Across the street, "street vendors" call out to travelers who slalom between the buses to get to the metro. A little further on, on the sidewalk, the demonstration of a mechanical toy attracts the attention of a young mother, who engages in bitter haggling, while the smell of grilled corn tickles her nose. These smells mingle with those of the exhaust pipes, but also with other ambient factors such as the sound of horns, which arouse all our senses.

The atmosphere is set. This orchestration of flows draws an improbable urban choreography which gives this intersection its singularity. Tango, ballet, waltz, macarena, The Madison, the intersection sets a tempo... not always easy to follow. At the "Quatre-Chemins", mobility has "style". There is a great temptation to denounce incivilities as a source of insecurity and to reduce this "bazaar" to anarchy. Let's go beyond this normative approach and try to understand the spirit of the place. Contrary to appearances, this is not anarchy, but rather a Brownian movement, in which everyone has learned to adjust in real time, according to the circumstances. "Quatre-Chemins" becomes the expression of a spontaneous urbanity that has its own harmony, its own logic of operation. It is also a platform for exchange that allows us to observe new informal and itinerant sales practices called "ambulantage". These practices inform us about our societies that have become increasingly nomadic... and globalized.

"Quatre-Chemins" is above all an intersection that resists the ambient conformism that consists in believing that we could regulate our behavior with algorithms. Freedom of movement is punctuated by these lines of code that program the traffic lights in order to optimize flow and reduce our carbon footprint. While there is no question here of questioning the indisputable technological advances that allow us to better regulate the flows and, more broadly, the consumption of our cities, an intersection cannot be reduced to its technical architecture and its digital matrix. The city is more complex. Intelligence is not an artifice. It is a human activity that is based precisely on this principle of adjustment to the context. A city, like an intersection, is a subtle play of tensions between the binary and the imaginary, between norms and uses, between practice and theory, between the source code of the "smart" city and the user codes of the "pop" city, which is based on a form of poaching. "Quatre-Chemins" is witness to this.

In the end, intersections should not be seen solely as a traffic machine. It is in fact a cultural space that has its own codes of (good) behavior that refer to implicit rules of use. Our intersections are organized around "rites" that vary according to the ambient factors and the socio-styles of the communities that frequent them... Here, the rites of passage become rites of transgression, a way of denouncing the mechanical management of our cities. These rites make intersections the reflection of a mosaic of atmospheres and a source of identity that make cities endearing in many ways. In sum: "Quatre-Chemins" is an anthropological object that deserves our attention because its functioning questions our own relationship to the world, to otherness, to diversity, and more specifically to the city. Let's listen to its message: if our intersections, that is, our movements, were regulated solely by algorithms, our cities would become uniform, homogeneous, and routine. Quatre-Chemins forcefully reminds us that an intersection is also a public space on which spontaneous practices are transplanted, which have the secret of micro-arrangements. It is in this way that it becomes the intersection of our humanities, a sensory space, a support for freedom, even for demands... which can transform the intersection, on certain occasions, into a public square anywhere in the world!

VOLVO

IV
EACH SQUARE HAS ITS OWN CHOREOGRAPHY

We have observed variations that are related to differences between movement cultures and site configurations. They provide information on the possibilities of crossing in a situation of high urban traffic. It is thus a question of the intensity of activity and the mix in the city. The combination of approaches to flows and their functioning, to the attitudes of mobile users and to the composition and organization of space and time, provide transversal keys for the evolution of functional intersections in urban places. We propose to use these criteria according to the context to reconfigure spaces abandoned to flows. Solutions emerge with a combination of movements and multiple passages per place. The principles presented below propose tools for choreographing squares.

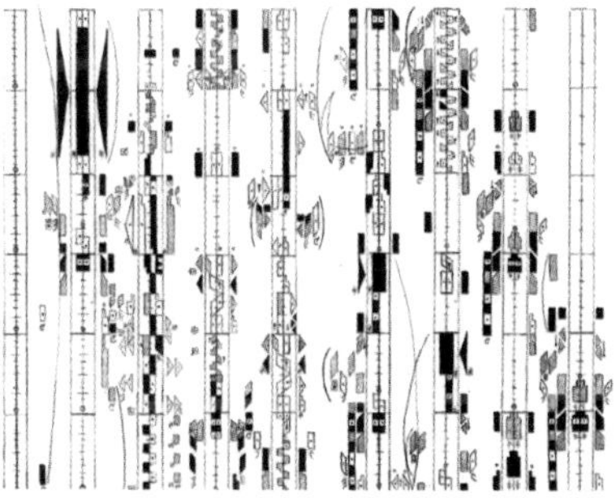

Example of a score using the Laban notation system, kinetography, Laban, Rudolph (1879-1958)

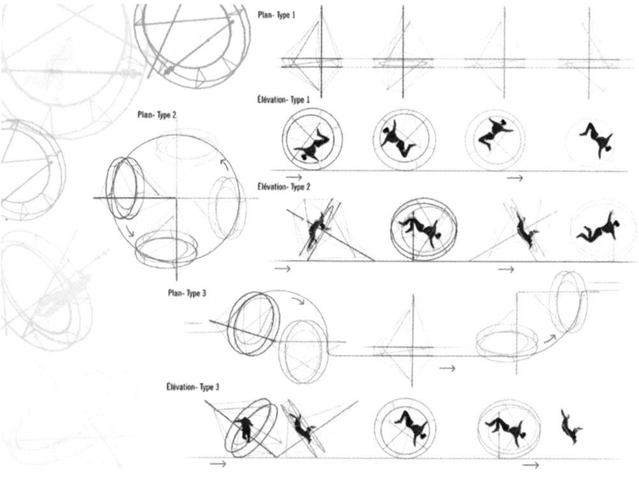

Typology of Non-Utility Vehicle Movements, 2020, Compagnie Retouramont and Stéphane Lemoine.

Maneuverability and the quantity of mobile elements as a regulator

The first criterion concerns the flexibility and reactivity of mobile elements. The more maneuverable they are, the greater the diversity of modes can be. Indeed, the design of the turning capacities for the change of direction is indicative of the flexibility of movements and crossings, between the pedestrian who can make a U-turn on the spot and the truck and the bus which are very limited in their movement (see the "butterfly" diagram, opposite page).

This integration capacity is also coupled with a maximum amount of mobile elements in the available public spaces. Taking into account the reaction time for braking and the minimum traffic spaces, some spaces are saturated beyond a certain number of vehicles.

These two constraints will play an important role in the reconfigurations and movements allowed in the intersection. The smaller the vehicle, the more skillful and numerous it can be to move through the public space. In addition, if the maximum quantities are exceeded based on the available space and the mix of mobile elements, it is necessary to limit traffic.

Afterwards, it is a question of ensuring that movements are possible between them.

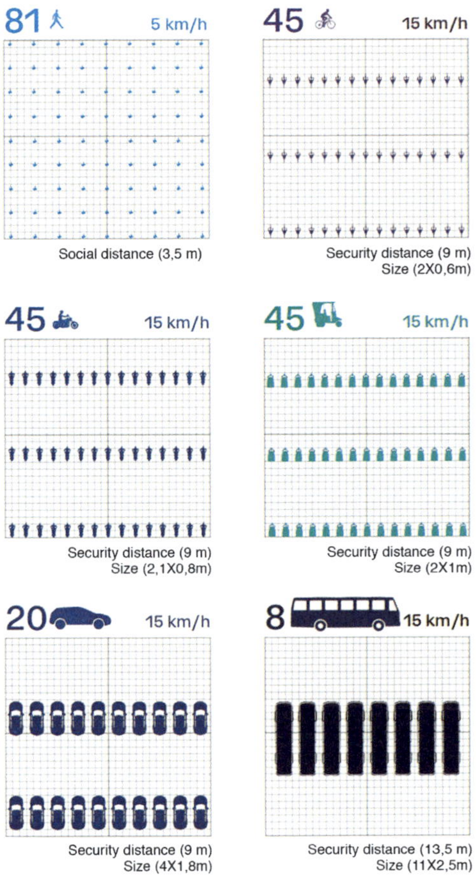

QUANTITATIVE GRID
capacity according to mobile elements on a 30mx30m space

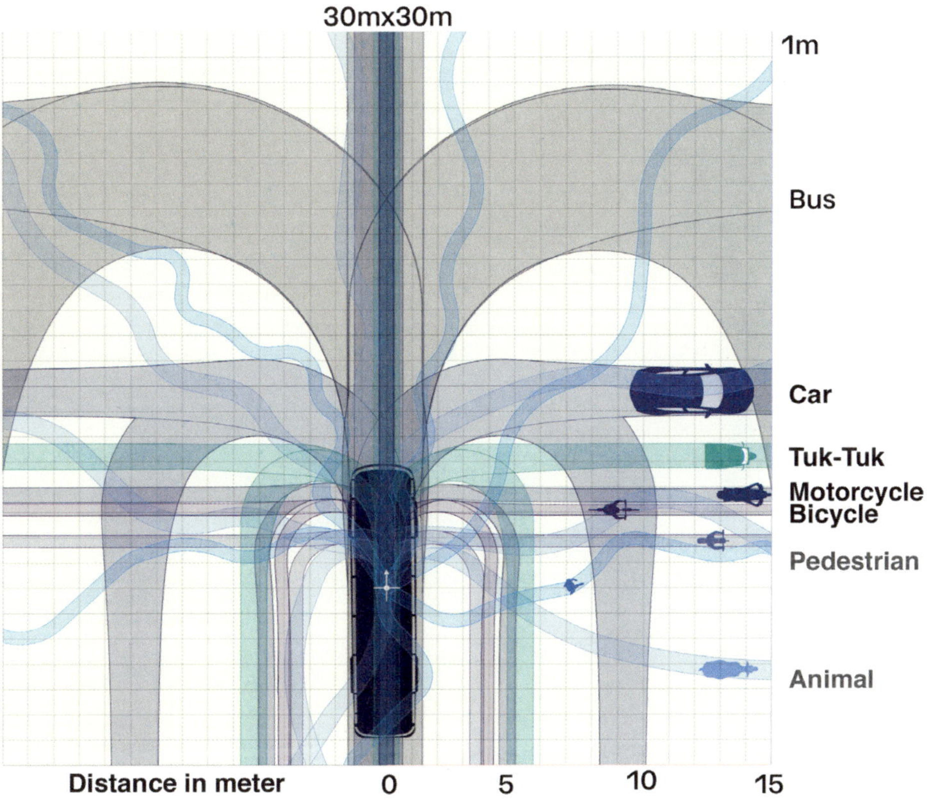

BUTTERFLY
The maneuverability of the mobile elements to turn right and left, or to turn around.

Crossing rules change routes and modal priorities

While the modal shares show a high degree of diversity in India, Africa and Asia, multi-modality is more limited in the other sites. Indeed, a dozen modes of transport are present in India, including animals, whereas in Denmark three main types are present: cars, bicycles, and pedestrians. Each case shows a strong distinction between cities based on the Western model, with a separation of flows and strict management, and cities in emerging countries, where flows and modes are very mixed. Thus, the management of flows with less control stands out when there is a strong multi-modality. This diversity is reflected in the very different types of movements at each site. Red light timing is replaced by a slower or irregular movement depending on the case.

The integration of the diversity of speeds (London case) and rhythms (Chinese case) allows an increased multi-modality and priority changes. Thus, the choice of speeds imposed on the different travel modes determines the level of multi-modality.

This multi-mode capacity is transferred onto the atmosphere of the urban spaces. The activity of the public square is as important as the safety towards the vehicles in movement.

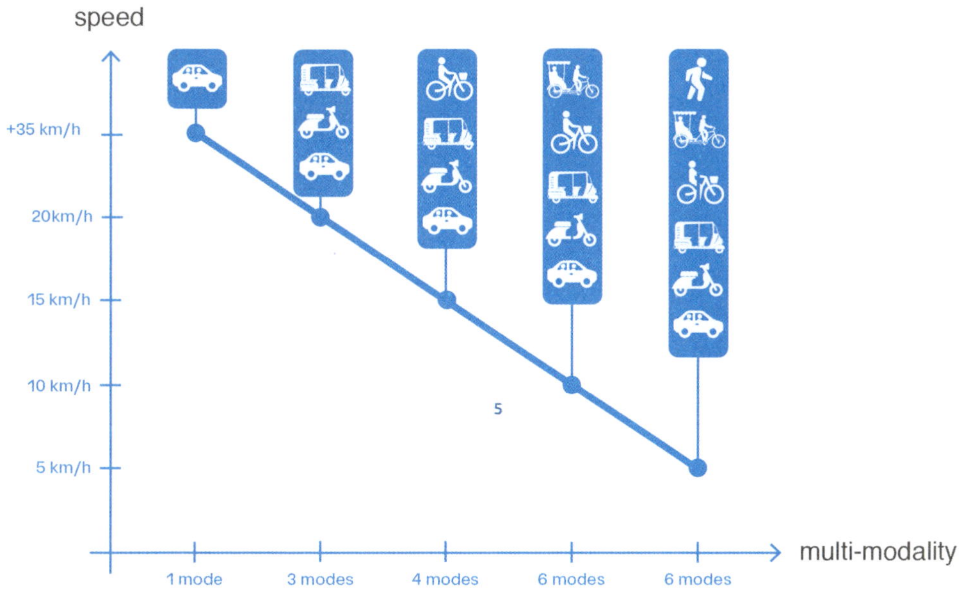

DEPENDENCE
The relationship between speed and the number of modes of travel

Attitudes that provide solutions for urban squares

What is possible in Hanoi is unthinkable in Denmark. Not only because of the distribution of modes of transport or urban configurations, but also because habits, discipline, civility and travel speeds are different. Crossing codes are enforced, semi-free or free depending on the site. The sequencing of red-light phases, adding a time for pedestrians, shows that different modal priorities are taken into account, as in London and Tokyo. Another case regarding the nature of movements, the traffic blocking at the semi-automated intersection in Lagos, shows stops of several minutes. At one point, with the development of street vendors who are very reactive in traffic jams, the exchange takes the upper hand from the crossing. This changeover is an interesting lead to explore according to the sites.

In Sao Paulo, the intersections are based on an orthogonal grid with no left turns. The freedom of movement is low but the speed is high, making it acceptable. In Old Delhi, the freedom is greater for the intersections, but very slowed down with the numerous possible crossings. These different ways of moving are indicative of different cultures that accept certain compromises in movement. These different attitudes allow for a great variety of movements. The freedom of reaction appears necessary for the quality of a crossing for the user. The possibility of having several trajectories is necessary for the appreciation of a public place. It is a question of going from the tunnel, without alternative, to a plateau with a minimum of freedom of direction.

The different attitudes to suggest are a source of design for intersections. These adjustment variables must be integrated to allow and maintain welcoming urban squares, where encounters are encouraged. The aim is to make possible the greatest possible diversity in the trajectories of mobile people, and to do this, all the handlings for crossings must be taken into account. The diversity of trajectories that must be integrated into the design of a public space that allows for exchange is specified in the adjacent table.

A maximum of diversity is to be guaranteed for the trajectories on a square.

CROSSOVER TRAJECTORIES
from red light to exchange

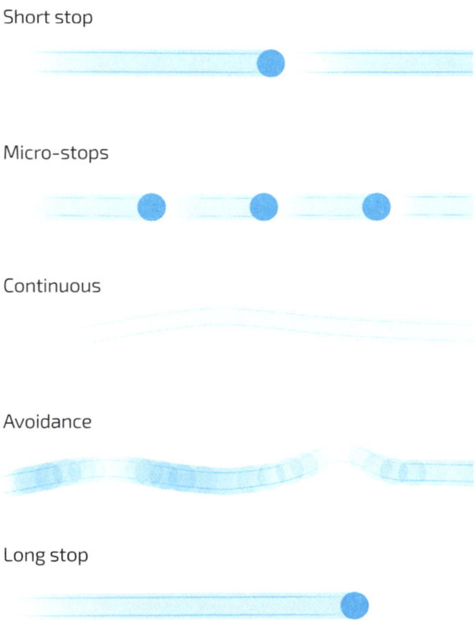

TRAJECTORIES ON THE SQUARE
multiple choreographies

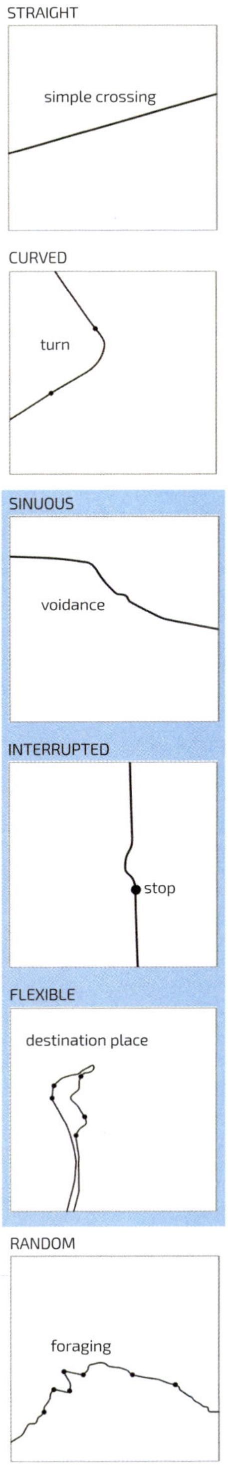

A maximum of diversity is to be guaranteed for the trajectories on a square.

The choreographies draw the urban mix

The observation is technical for understanding the rules laid down for each crossing and the modal distribution, but it is also sensitive with the recording of the variety of movements observed and the atmosphere resulting from the crossings. The relationship with the other in the public space is the result of possible movements. The whole draws choreographies specific to each site. The representation of the routes with a color for each speed makes it possible to see the combination of movements for each intersection. These illustrations show differences for all the movements that take place. This qualification of the intersections provides information on the possible variables for urban spaces, beyond the solutions of the roundabout or the traffic light. The combination of movements gives very rich statements. This can become a set of objectives to be achieved in order to talk about urbanity. It is a question of trajectories that graze each other and no longer of abstract line crossings.[24]

Speeds are to be slowed down, crossings are to be multiplied, in number and mode, and the forms of trajectories are to be freed up as much as possible. With a composition of the diversity of movements, spaces and temporalities, public spaces are qualified by including new practices. The design of squares becomes a choreography over several minutes to be articulated with the calendar of longer temporalities (week, seasons, years) and spatial constraints.

This essay suggests the careful and attentive urban mix to appreciate and design urban squares. The overview opposite shows the combination of intersection types depending on the roads (from paths to highways) and the passage variations for the crossing phases. The calmest and most urban intersections are found in intermediary typologies. The movements are the most diversified.

24 Ingold, Tim, 2007, Lines: *A Brief History*, London, Routledge .

Qualitative matrix

Give time to crossings and comfort

Following the case study and this search for urban criteria for the quality of the square, the characteristics to be retained are:

- Quiet, alternating, and multiple movements to ensure user comfort,
- Increased time phasing to accommodate more directions and modes,
- Supports designed with calm and intense spaces to integrate into the city and its polarity.

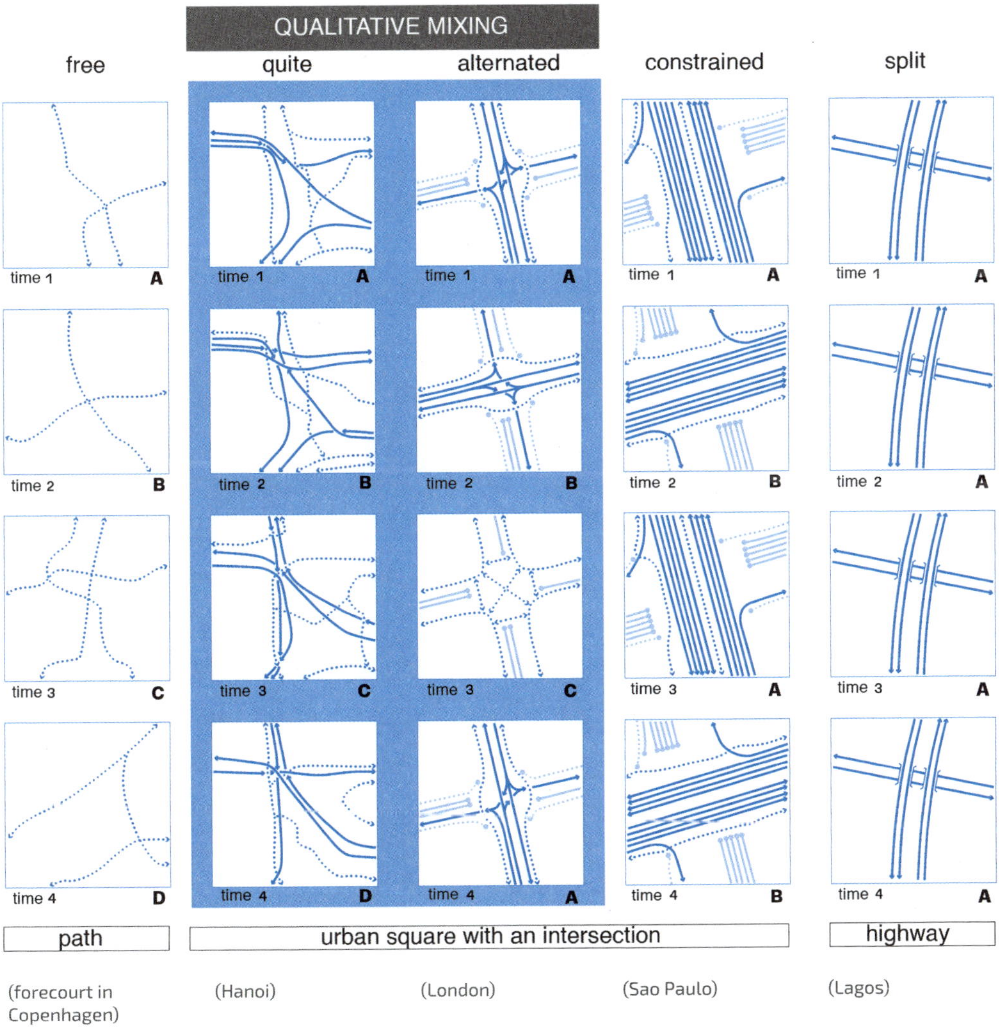

CONDITIONS FOR URBAN SQUARES

Below, we propose some conditions for an intersection to become a square following our survey:

- the site is a destination,
- the organization of crossings takes into account the number of participants (quantity) and local practices (multi-modality),
- the sharing of public space at intersections integrates as many modes of transport as possible (minimum 3),
- traffic management includes time phasing for several modes,
- mobility services are part of the management of the intersection,
- the ability to stop and change course and speed are mandatory for the pedestrian,
- the possibility of speed and trajectory variation increases the freedom of movement for mobile people and is a priority for pedestrians,
- the public space of the intersection welcomes practices other than passage, with breaks, exchanges (bartering, trade, words...), festivities, the unexpected, plants, water and flora,
- the practices are simultaneous and alternative,
- speed, distance, and cost are no longer the measurable indicators for the urban quality of a square, it becomes the diversity (multiplicity and complexity) of possible movements,
- speed is limited for all, so as to increase multi-modality and safety.

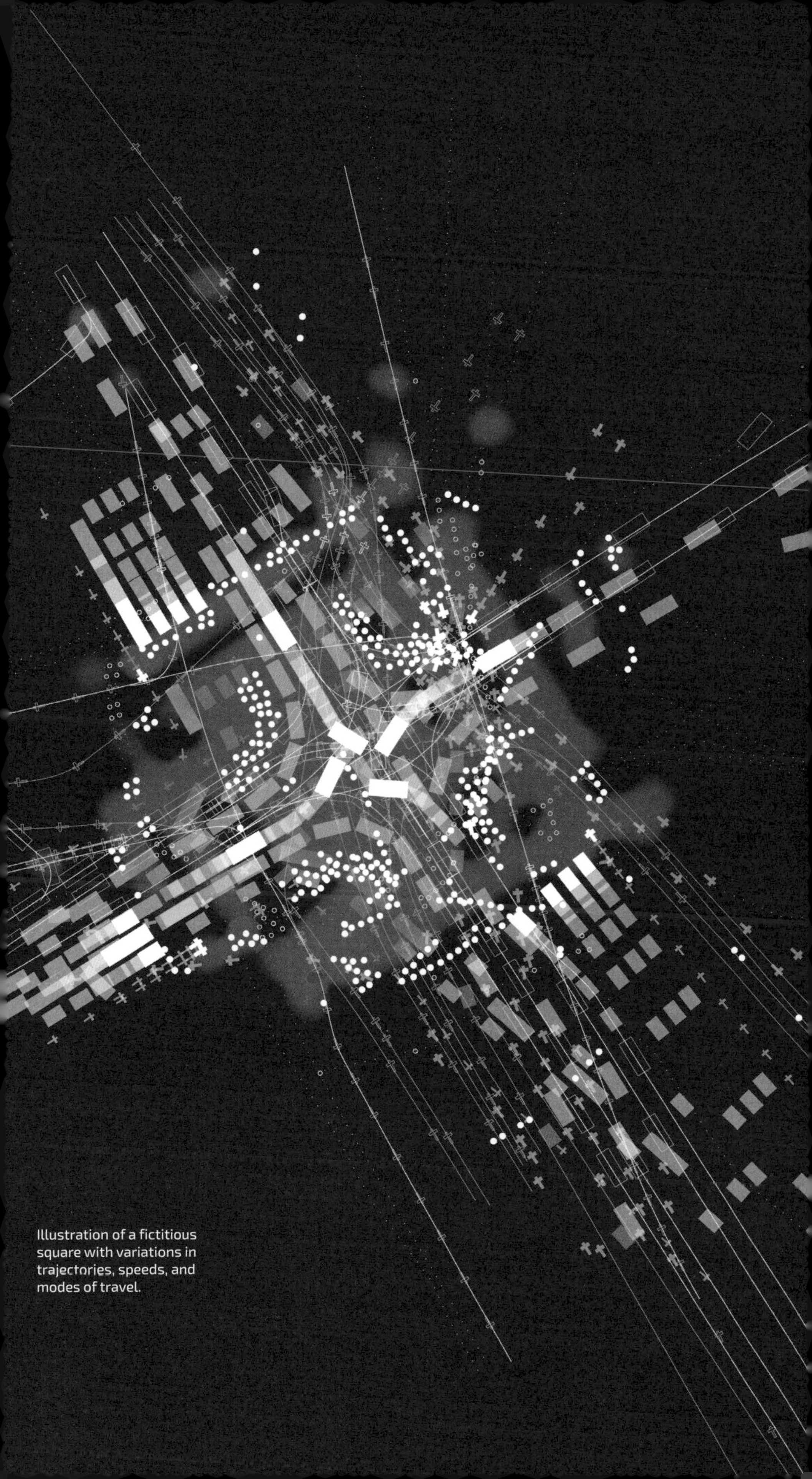

Illustration of a fictitious square with variations in trajectories, speeds, and modes of travel.

The above survey presents reactive practices that require the participation of inhabitants and the involvement of an attentive territorial governance. The governance of the city has the power to promote mobility by ensuring the diversity of movements. Whether it is the reconfiguration of urban spaces, the development of local habitats and exchanges, energy management, or the modification of the sharing of public space, it is vital to change the criteria for evaluating these everyday spaces. Neighborhood and metropolitan administrators are responsible for these spaces of intersections abandoned to the car and in conflict with the city. The diversity of movements is a richness of the city to be organized and developed.

Even if the quantitative aspect is not to be excluded, it is about changing the values retained. We propose to retain a high level of crossing, rather than passage, and a large number of types of movement, below which the intersection would not have urban status, but machine status. For each of the users, of the modes of movement, the choices, according to the contexts, cannot go below two alternatives of direction and speed. These conditions are the basis for making intersections more welcoming.

For the qualitative dimension of urban public spaces, described for several millennia by philosophers as the places of individuals in society and the city,[25] we recall here the approach of Yvan Illich,[26] who advocates that man must retain control of the devices he puts in place. The necessary approach of the managers of the city's spaces – centered on proper functioning (fluidity and quantity), on the economy of means and on avoidance (security) – must not crush the programs, the devices and the organizations that allow attention be given to the person we cross, to the site and to exchanges. The forms explored above throughout the world are all examples that show the possibility of meeting according to one's culture of space and relationship to the other. The functioning of a crossroads is not unique, as it can be multiple and hybrid, by mixing the examples visited. Slowing down allows one to adjust one's trajectory, to appreciate the place one is crossing, to stop. The mixture of attitudes explored shows a diversity of movements, often forgotten or unknown, which allow new interactions between users of a public space. The urban and reactive mix makes it possible to imagine new urbanizations through the architecture of intersections.

Precedent page:
Decomposition of movements on a fictional crossroads.

25 For the most recent, see Anne Cauquelin, with l'Invention du Paysage, 2002, Paris, PUF, which questions the nature of spaces and perception, or Joelle Zask with *Se réunir, du rôle des places dans la cité*, 2022, Paris, *Premier Parallèle Poche*, which draws a portrait of the public square with its symbols and activities since ancient Greece.

26 Illitch, Yvan, 1975, *La Convivialité*, Collection Points.

BEING ATTENTIVE AND REACTIVE TO THE PERSON CROSSED IN A SPECIFIC TIME INTERVAL IS A PREREQUISITE FOR THE URBANITY OF THE CITY'S INHABITANTS, JUST LIKE THE ABILITY OF A SURFER TO ADAPT HIMSELF TO THE WAVE WITH WHICH HE WILL BE ABLE TO MOVE. IT'S RELATIVE MOTION.

Selected bibliography

Urbanism

- Benjamin, Walter, 1934 (1989 vf). *Paris, capitale du XIXe siècle, Le livre des passages*, Paris, Le Cerf.

- Lynch, Kevin, 1969 (1989 vf), *l'image de la cité*, Paris, Dunod.

- Benevolo, Leonardo, 1975 (2000 vf), *Histoire de la ville*, Paris Eyrolles.

- Webber, Melvin, 1996, *L'urbain sans lieu ni bornes*, La Tour d'Aigues, éd de L'aube (translation from "The Urban Place and the Nonplace Urban Realm", 1963).

- Whyte, William H., 1980, *The Social Life of Small Urban Spaces.* Washington D.C., The Conservation Foundation, 125p. First surveys in the 1970s on the atmosphere with the survey of pedestrian traffic

- Appleyard, Donald, 1980, *Livable Streets, protected neighborhood?* the annals of the American academy of Political and social science.

- Rivkin, Jérémy, 2005, *L'âge de l'accès*, Paris, La découverte.

- Gayet-Viaud, Carole, 2022, *La civilité urbaine, Les formes élémentaires de la coexistence démocratique*, Economica, collection études sociologiques

- Gehl, Jan, 2013, *For Cities on a Human Scale*, Montreal, Ecosociety Publishing.

- Mongin, Olivier, 2013, *La ville des flux*, Paris, Fayard.

- Alonzo, Eric, 2018, *L'architecture de la voie.* Histoire et théories. Marseille, Parenthèses.

- Offner, Jean-Marc, 2020, *Anachronismes urbains*, Presses de SciencesPo.

Mobilities

- Hénard, Eugène, 1906, *Les Voitures et les passants Carrefours libres et carrefours à giration*, Etudes sur les transformations de Paris par... Fasc. 7... Paris: Librairie impr. réunies.

- Kaufmann, Vincent, 2002, "Temps et pratiques modales. Is the shorter the better?", Transport Safety Research, Editions scientifiques et médicales Elsevier SAS and INRETS.

- Ascher, François, Appel-Muller Mireille, 2007, *La rue est à nous tous*, international exhibition, Institut de la ville en mouvement.

- Charleux, L. and Chardonnel S., 2009, *Génération automatisée de visualisations animées pour l'exploration des trajectoires individuelles de mobilité: guider l'intuition dans l'analyse de données complexes*, Neuvièmes Rencontres de ThéoQuant, Besançon.

- Amar, Georges, 2010, *Homo Mobilis, Une civilisation du mouvement*, Fyp edition.

- Gay, Christophe, Kaufmann, Vincent, Landière Sylvie, Vincent-Geslin Stéphanie, (eds.). 2011. *Mobile/immobile*, Forum vies Mobiles. L'aube.

- Lemoine, Stéphane, 2015, *Ville et Voiture, l'échelle humaine des déplacements*, p.160, coll. under the direction of A. Masboungi, Le Moniteur.

- Institut Paris Région, Les déterminants du choix modal, synthesis of scientific knowledge, February 2020, digital distribution https://www.institutparisregion.fr/nos-travaux/publications/les-determinants-du-choix-modal/

Représentations des flux

- Hagerstrand, T. 1970, "Wha about People in Regional Science", Papers of the Regio Science Association 24, 6–21

- Tufte, Edward. 2001, *The Visual Display of Quantitativ Information* / 1990, Envisioni Information, USA, Graphics Press.

- Mc Quaid, *Envisioning Architecture*, 2003, New York MOMA.

- Klanten Robert, Bourquin Nicolas, Tissot Thibaud, Ema Svent, 2009, *Data Flow*, Than & Hudson, Paris

- Arnall, Timo: www.elasticspace.com. *Wireless. Robot readable world.* 2010.

- Lemoine, Stéphane, 2015, *Composing urban flows, Proceedings of the symposiu on flow modelling for urban planning*, Lille Grand Palais, Ministry of the Environment, Advancity, IFSTTAR, Universit of Lille.

- Felton, Nicolas, 2016, *Photo Visualizing Information throu Photography*, Berlin, Gestalte

Anthropology

- Descola Phillipe, 2021, *Les formes du visible, une anthropologie de la figuratior* Paris, Seuil.

- Hall, E.T., 1971 (1966), La Dimension cachée, Paris, Seui

- Goffman Erwing, 1973 (2018 vf), *La mise en scène de la vie quotidienne, 2. Relations in Public* Paris, Minuit.

- Illitch, Yvan, 1975, *La Convivialité*, Collection Points

- Ingold Tim, 2011, *Une brève histoire des lignes*, Brussels,

- Jarrigeon Anne, 2009, *La Villette - vies, Synchronies et polyrythmies d'un parc urbain extrait de Ambiances urbaines en partage : pour une écologie sociale de la ville sensible*, ss la direction de Thibaud, Jean Paul, Rose Cristiane, 2013, Geneva, MétisPresses.

Sources on the internet 2020

India
https://www.youtube.com/watch?v=FmMN0KvD0Sg&t=259s
https://www.youtube.com/watch?v=fXa8wZDsaqA
https://www.youtube.com/watch?v=-0jEuw-8GeA&t=127s
https://www.youtube.com/watch?v=0KfkbidW6g4

Denmark
https://www.youtube.com/watch?v=Wt-WYrXmcUM -
https://www.youtube.com/watch?v=996Hg2GeUvo&t=13s
https://www.webcamtaxi.com/en/denmark/capital-region-of-denmark/copenhagen-city-centre.html

Japan
https://worldcams.tv/japan/tokyo/shibuya-crossing
https://www.youtube.com/watch?v=QXt0dSgf6lc
https://www.amusingplanet.com/2016/11/tokyos-iconic-shibuya-crossing.html-
https://www.youtube.com/watch?v=Nw4GRjAeE-A
https://www.youtube.com/watch?v=5ffj92FJY0c

Vietnam
http://goldencyclohotel.com/hanoi-night-market-nd16224.html?lang=en
https://www.youtube.com/watch?v=Uz5uxAsrbwI&t=131s
https://www.youtube.com/watch?v=LXH77nw-1bk
https://www.youtube.com/watch?v=Gf8_lzCWvq4
https://www.youtube.com/watch?v=dIFku4gJmho
https://www.youtube.com/watch?v=as8lRafELrc

London
https://www.youtube.com/watch?v=Aw-6OSCnHA0
https://www.youtube.com/watch?v=AyZn6r0cZQA
https://www.youtube.com/watch?v=jNti6yZ5oeY
https://www.shutterstock.com/fr/video/clip-14657242-london-oxford-circus-christmas-time-street-view
https://www.windy.com/-Webcams/United-Kingdom/England/London/Oxford-Circus/wwebcams/1508414460?51.509,-13.315,5
http://www.camvista.com/england/london/traffic-cameras-tfl-jam-webcams-london-oxford-street-davies-street/index.php
https://www.trafficdelays.co.uk/oxford-circus-london-cctv-traffic-cameras/

Nigeria
https://www.youtube.com/watch?v=UhvqmEjApSM
https://www.youtube.com/watch?v=7bs7YaDCtuA
https://www.youtube.com/watch?v=yEVDl7jUNyA
https://www.youtube.com/watch?v=yEVDl7jUNyA
https://www.youtube.com/watch?v=-d_-de8TP9U
https://autojosh.com/the-beautification-of-under-ojuelegba-bridge-has-the-project-been-abandoned-photos/
https://www.shutterstock.com/fr/video/clip-1032890000-30-june-2019-lagos-nigeria-under-bridge
https://www.shutterstock.com/fr/video/clip-1033471919-30-june-2019-lagos-nigeria-heavy-duty
https://www.shutterstock.com/fr/video/clip-1043360143-surulere-lagos-state-nigeria-africa---july
https://www.shutterstock.com/fr/video/clip-26581007-busy-nigerian-market-lagos-nigeria---april

Brazil
https://www.shutterstock.com/fr/video/clip-28180795-top-view-faria-lima-x-juscelino-kubitschek
https://www.istockphoto.com/in/video/top-view-of-faria-lima-x-juscelino-kubitschek-avenue-in-sao-paulo-brazil-gm863656602-143698147
https://www.youtube.com/watch?v=nfD5Czc9Ey4
https://www.youtube.com/watch?v=0qDxlgqLDw0&has_verified=1

China
https://www.youtube.com/watch?v=7J4kQ7TmMN4
https://www.youtube.com/watch?v=DNjCX4kMgh8
crossing nect the chosen square
https://www.youtube.com/watch?v=fn5RJK5qcxE
https://www.youtube.com/watch?v=p4Xx2zCiq04

+ visualisations sur le site Googlemaps©2020-2022

Thanks to:

Corinne Tiry-Ono, Julia Tanski, Patrick Henry, Philippe Massé, Stéphane Juguet, Fabrice Guillot, Eric Alonzo, Marc Salomon, Bui Quang Tuan, Georges Amar, Laurent Burte, Étienne Leblanc, Ricardo Devesa, Marta Bugés and Gema Mila.

Urban Mix

Explorations of 8 Crossings around the World : Movements & Interactions

Published by
Actar Publishers, New York, Barcelona
www.actar.com

Authors
Stéphane Lemoine (design and text) and Sophie Harache (drawings)

Edited by
AP5, Agence d'architecture, de paysage et d'urbanisme © Paris, France
https://www.ap5.fr

Graphic design
AP5 / Actar

With contributions from
Stephane Lemoine, Sophie Harache, Anisha Suri, Jeanne Vincent, Philippe Massé, Ameshi Shrivastava, Fabrice Guillot, Stephane Juguet, and Eric Alonzo

French-English translation
Julia Tanski

Printing and binding
Arlequin SL

Image credits:
P4: Tokyo / Japan Shibuya crossing by Marcel Schaufelberger / x-frame.ch.
P7: Lagos / Nigeria, Ojuelegba and Alagbede-Igbobi Road and A1 intersection by OMONIYI AYEDUN OLUBUNMI / Alamy Stock Photo.
P52: Hanoi / Vietnam, Dong Kinh Nghia Thuc Square, by Bui Quang Tuan, 2022.
P76: Old Delhi / India Hauz Qasi Chowk, by Ameeshi Shrivastava, 2022.
P90-91: Biarritz/ France, Beach Cote des Basques, by Stéphane Lemoine, 2020.
P94: London / England Oxford Circus, by Waterfold_Man, 2016.

Distribution
Actar D, Inc. New York, Barcelona

New York
440 Park Avenue South, 17th Floor
New York, NY 10016, USA
T +1 2129662207
salesnewyork@actar-d.com

Barcelona
Roca and Batlle 2-4
08023 Barcelona, Spain
T +34 933 282 183
eurosales@actar-d.com

Indexing
English ISBN: 978-1-63840-058-5
LCCN: 2022944865

Printed in Europe

Release date: April 2023

Available in French
French ISBN : 978-1-63840-059-2